D1366244

Enhancing Student Learning

ACPA Media Board

Stan Carpenter, Editor/Chair
Texas A & M University

Janice Sutera Wolfe, Associate Editor
George Mason University

Philip E. Burns, Commissions Chair Representative
University of Nevada, Los Vegas

Eric Anderson
Capital University

Rosa Cintron
University of Oklahoma

Alan Farber
Northern Illinois University

Hilton Hallock
Syracuse University

Jeanne Higbee
University of Georgia

Fiona MacKinnon-Slaney
Bowling Green State University

Alan "Woody" Schwitzer
Old Dominion University

Cynthia Straub
Washtenaw Community College

Saundra Tomlison-Clarke
Rutgers University

ACPA Central Office Liaison:
Donna M. Bourassa

Enhancing Student Learning

Setting the Campus Context

Editors

Frances K. Stage
Lemuel W. Watson
Melvin Terrell

American College Personnel Association

Copyright © 1999 by
The American College Personnel Associations

University Press of America,® Inc.
4720 Boston Way
Lanham, Maryland 20706

12 Hid's Copse Rd.
Cumnor Hill, Oxford OX2 9JJ

All rights reserved
Printed in the United States of America
British Library Cataloging in Publication Information Available

Library of Congress Cataloging-in-Publication Data

Enhancing student learning : setting the campus context /editors,
Frances K. Stage, Lemuel W. Watson, Melvin Terrell.
p. cm.
Includes bibliographical references.
College student development programs—United States. 2. College
students—United States—Psychology. 3. Education, Higher—Aims
and objectives—United States. 4. Learning, Psychology of. 5.
College teaching—United States. 6. Student affairs services—
United States. I. Stage, Frances K. II. Watson, Lemuel W.
(Lemuel Warren) III. Terrell, Melvin C.
LB2343.4.E54 1999 370.15'23—dc21 98-51299 CIP

ISBN 1-883485-15-0 (cloth: alk. ppr.)
ISBN 1-883485-16-9 (pbk: alk. ppr.)

♾™ The paper used in this publication meets the minimum
requirements of American National Standard for Information
Sciences—Permanence of Paper for Printed Library Materials,
ANSI Z39.48—1984

Dedication

This book is dedicated to Robert H. Shaffer who has provided and continues to provide rich inspiration for thousands of student affairs professionals.

Contents

Enhancing Student Learning

Frances K. Stage
Lemuel W. Watson
Melvin Terrell

A focus on connections between learning and student affairs is not new (Banning, 1989; Blimlimg and Schuh, 1981; Brown, 1968, 1989; DeCoster, 1968; Greenleaf, Forsythe, Godfrey, Hudson, and Thompson, 1967; Schroeder, 1973), but it is perhaps more urgent given the current higher education climate. Resources that seemed tight through the eighties became almost nonexistent in the nineties. Often the burden of cuts to colleges and universities was shifted from academic units to student affairs and other departments that were considered supportive but not central to the academic mission. Additionally, demands for accountability by legislators, trustees, parents, and students put pressure on all aspects of college life. Today as never before student affairs and academic units must demonstrate their centrality to undergraduate education and their unique contributions to student learning.

The student affairs profession is now renewing efforts to demonstrate its many contributions to undergraduate education (Chickering and Gamson, 1987; Chickering and Reisser, 1993; Schroeder, 1993;

1

Schroeder and Mable, 1994). *The Student Learning Imperative* in particular (American College Personnel Association, 1994), has focused increased attention on the important role student affairs educators can play in enhancing student learning and educational attainment.

As we address the learning needs of our campuses in an urgent fashion, we offer this monograph as a resource. We believe that as a profession we can benefit from new ways of looking at old problems as well as new ones. Additionally, we suggest that academic learning is equally important as our already strong focus on the personal development of college students (Stage, 1996).

This monograph provides student affairs professionals, college faculty, and educators of student affairs professionals with suggestions for the employment of a variety of theories relevant to the task of educating college students. Additionally, faculty and other academic professionals might find the approaches useful as they work to design programs and redesign courses for optimal student learning.

The first three chapters provide theoretical bases for the remaining chapters. We emphasize the importance of wholistic views of learning particularly now, when student populations have changed dramatically (Chapter 1). We describe the work of psychologists and others who depict learning in ways that are helpful as we seek to enhance learning on our campuses (Chapter 2). These theories form a link to the remaining chapters of the monograph. Chapter 3 addresses considerations of culture in student learning, involvement, and educational outcomes. In particular, theories focusing on learning styles and motivation to learn are examined with respect to specific diverse cultures.

Chapter 4 demonstrates theory to practice examples for a variety of theories relative to four specific campus outcomes. Theory to practice models are presented for these four particular challenges for student affairs professionals: facilitating learning, developing a sense of community, the use of value in learning and development, and developing a service ethic.

Chapter 5 reminds us that the community college setting is increasingly important and unique in providing opportunities for student learning and development. Particular institutional conditions, policies, and practices provide special challenges for student affairs professionals as they work toward the enhancement of student learning on their community college campuses. Service-learning provides an excellent example of a close linking of academic and student affairs professionals and is described as such in Chapter 6. The focus is on the application of psychological theory to this very specific student affairs venue that is of growing interest on college campuses.

Chapter 7 reminds us that assessment has become increasingly important not only for showing us how well we are doing and where we need to adjust, but also for demonstrating the importance of broad dimensions of the college campus to learning. Finally, we draw on all chapters to conclude with speculation about learning in a new campus context. As college campuses learn and grow they can expect to maximize their own students' change and development. We look toward the future as we build total learning environments on our campuses.

References

American College Personnel Association (ACPA) (1994). *The student learning imperative: Implications for student affairs*. Washington, DC: Author.

Banning, J. H. (1989). Creating a climate for successful student development: The campus ecology model. In U. Delworth, G. Hanson, and Associates (Eds.), *Student services: A handbook for the profession* (2nd ed.) San Francisco: Jossey-Bass.

Blimling, G. S. and Schuh, J. H. (1981). *Increasing the Educational Role of Residence Halls*. (New Directions for Student Services, No. 13) San Francisco: Jossey-Bass.

Brown, R. (1968). Manipulation of the environmental press in a college residence hall. *Personnel and Guidance Journal, 46*, 555–560.

Brown, R. (1989). Fostering intellectual and personal growth: The student development role. In U. Delworth, G. Hanson, and Associates, *Student services: A handbook for the profession*, (2nd ed.) San Francisco: Jossey-Bass.

Chickering, A. W. and Gamson, Z. F. (1987). Seven good practices in undergraduate education. *AAHE Bulletin, 39*(7), 3–7.

Chickering, A.W. and Reisser, L. (1993). *Education and identity* (2nd Ed.) San Francisco: Jossey-Bass.

DeCoster, D. (1968). Effects of homogeneous housing assignments for high ability students. *Journal of College Student Personnel, 8*, 75–78.

Greenleaf, E. A., Forsythe, M., Godfrey, H., Hudson, B., and Thompson, F. (1967). *Undergraduate students as members of the residence hall staff*. Bloomington, IN: National Association of Women Deans and Counselors.

Schroeder, C. C. (1973). Sex differences and growth toward self-actualization during the freshman year. *Psychological Reports, 32*, 416-418.

Schroeder, C. C. (1988). "Student affairs–academic affairs: Opportunities for bridging the gap." *ACPA Developments*, Fall.

Schroeder, C. C. (1993). New students—new learning styles. *Change, 25*(4), 21–26.

Schroeder, C. C. and Mable, P. (1994). *Realizing the educational potential of residence halls*. New Directions for Higher and Adult Education. San Francisco: Jossey-Bass.

Stage, F. K. (1996). Setting the context: Psychological theories of learning. *Journal of College Student Development, 27*(2), 227–235

1

A Framework to Enhance Student Learning

Lemuel W. Watson
Frances K. Stage

Learning is often viewed as the unifying goal of teaching, research, and service for higher education. The term is widely used and difficult to define precisely. Learning has been described as knowing and interpreting the known, discovering the new, and bringing about desired change in cognitive and affective skills and characteristics of individuals (Bowen, 1977). Domjan (1993) describes learning as a change in behavior that meets three criteria. First, students think, perceive, or react to the environment in a new way; second, change is the result of students' experiences in repetition, study, practices, or observations; third, the change is relatively permanent.

This chapter introduces a framework that can be used for planning and discussing the complexities and factors in designing a campus to enhance learning, involvement, and educational outcomes. Then, Chapter 2 explores student learning in depth across specific theories. Here we describe the framework briefly, then present a case study involving learning on a college campus. Next we present the three aspects of the framework in greater detail using the case study to demonstrate practical applications. Finally, we summarize and set the context for the remaining chapters.

Student Affairs and Learning

The literature in student affairs is derived from a variety of fields that includes psychology, anthropology, sociology, organizational development, and counseling. Over the last decade, involvement has increasingly become the focus of research on college students. Involvement is characterized by the time and energy students expend in interacting with the resources and agents of an institution, as well as the amount of physical and psychological energy that students commit to their educational experience. Research has demonstrated that involvement on campus in a variety of ways is intrinsically linked to learning (Astin 1984; Pace 1984; Pascarella and Terenzini, 1991).

How do those of us in higher education ensure that we are acting responsibly in our attempts to foster student learning? We suggest engaging in wholistic planning. That is, we can examine a multitude of factors and avenues in order to maximize students learning and educational gains. Wholistic planning requires professionals to address issues within systems, examining how one factor affects another, rather than addressing them in hierarchical order. It is important for us to evaluate the links between the curriculum, co-curriculum, programs, services, community, learning and other social systems simultaneously while identifying our professional responsibilities and boundaries.

Student affairs professionals support the notion of wholistic learning for students. For example, one professional association declares that while students are maturing intellectually, they are also developing physically, psychologically, socially, aesthetically, ethically, sexually, and spiritually (National Association of Student Personnel Administrators, 1987, p. 11). It is equally important that we consider how students develop across the above dimensions prior to their enrollment within institutions of higher education. Are we doing enough for our students in planning programs and services without considering data that would assist us in maximizing their involvement in college and their educational gains? More recently, the American College Personnel Association sponsored *The Student Learning Imperative: Implications for Student Affairs* (SLI) (ACPA, 1994) which attempted to refocus the student affairs professional's role in student learning.

Such challenges have resulted in debates on some campuses as to what roles student affairs professionals might take regarding their responsibilities toward students' learning. For example, one Midwestern institution integrated the (SLI) into the strategic plan of their student affairs units. However, during the process, debates evolved among student affairs professionals regarding whether they should call themselves "services providers" or "educators." Some student affairs professionals wondered what faculty would think about student affairs professionals calling themselves educators. The problem is not really what we call ourselves as much as what our purpose and mission are as they relate to students' learning and development. Yet, the way we perceive ourselves does have an impact on the responsibilities and commitment we demonstrate in programs and services for student learning. We must ask "do we know enough about students in order to create opportunities to motivate them to become involved and committed to their educational experience?" Because it is important to design environments with learning opportunities to cause growth and development for our students, we need to incorporate techniques to encourage us to think simultaneously about several factors that affect educational outcomes.

A Conceptual Framework for Student Learning, Involvement, and Gains

Watson (1994, 1996) drew from Pace's (1984) and Astin's (1984) work to develop a conceptual framework for student learning, involvement, and gains. His model was designed to encourage a critical perspective for professionals when planning and addressing students' learning (see Figure 1). While the model employs familiar theoretical concepts, it is unique in proposing a simple and practical framework to spark a wholistic, creative, systematic, and critical thinking process that may be applied by student affairs professionals for enhancing student learning in the co-curriculum. The conceptual framework can be used as a planning tool. The framework is composed of three basic, dynamic, and interactive components.

- Input – Includes characteristics and experiences that students bring with them to college. We seem to do a great job of examining GPAs and standardized test scores; however we know little about students as we move away from these factors. For example, students' experiences in secondary institutions, home and community environments, as well as their age, gender, marital status, college class, housing,

Figure 1

Conceptual Framework for Student Learning, Involvement, and Gains

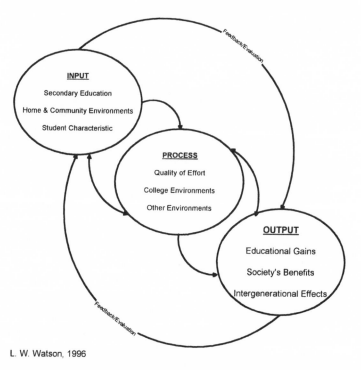

L. W. Watson, 1996

Figure 1. A conceptual framework for student learning, involvement, and gains. [L.W. Watson, 1996]

major, parents' schooling, and race all influence their college experience. As we will discover in Chapter 2, the importance of self-efficacy, students' beliefs about their capabilities, and those effects on their lives before, during, and after college all are powerful factors in the educational experience.

- Process – Includes behavioral involvement of students on campus; quality of effort and time spent (in scholarly and intellectual activities, informal personal activities, use of group facilities, organizational activities); and influences from the college environment (agents, peers, resources, and places on-campus where students expend time and energies). Other environments represent agents, peers, resources, and places off-campus where students might spend their time and energies. These spaces may include off-campus housing, churches, community centers, bars, and sports centers. Chapters 2, 3 and 4 explore the rationale for considering students, how they view themselves and how and why they choose to become involved both on and off the campus.

- Output – Represents educational gains in personal, social, intellectual, vocational, and cultural preparation while attending an institution of higher education (Pace, 1988) as well as societal benefits and intergenerational effects. The literature on educational outcomes is plentiful. We know that as students proceed through college they develop along many dimensions (Pascarella and Terenzini, 1991). Central to most development theories is the notion of identity, those values and principles by which students live their lives. Raising consciousness to a higher level of understanding regarding the value of and respect for human existence, both collective and individual, is a major contribution to society.

In simple terms, this framework demonstrates the relationships and the influences that multiple factors may have on learning. When planning programs and services, we can consider how the program may interact with each component of the framework, input, process, and output; in addition, the opportunity should exist for program and service improvement through an evaluation or feedback process. Assessment and evaluation are the only means by which we, as professionals, can demonstrate the effectiveness of our efforts for students' growth and development. The importance of assessment and evaluation and the ways in which they may be approached are discussed in more detail by Upcraft in Chapter 7. In Figure 1 the student's characteristics as input can play an important role in how an individual perceives him or herself within the college environment (input). In addition, the student's characteristics also may determine the quality of effort (process) with institutional agents and resources. Students are also involved in and with various off campus activities and other environments (process) that affect the quality of effort while in college. Finally, students' characteristics, college environment, and quality of effort all have direct effects on educational gains (output).

Our conceptual framework provides student affairs professionals with a creative and critical way of thinking about the learning styles and theories of college students. The framework is designed to facilitate the use of theories in practical settings and to enhance the relationship between student affairs professionals and other units on and off the college campus. The conceptual framework highlights the importance of partnerships between high schools, two-year, and four-year institutions; the diversity of students, their learning styles and those effects on educational outcomes; and the training of future student affairs professionals to integrate the skills needed to enhance and create an environment where learning is maximized for each student. Below we describe the three major components of the model while incorporating a practical example to demonstrate the application of the conceptual framework in the campus context. First, the case:

Central State University (CSU) was established in 1901 as a state normal school and is now a comprehensive public university controlled by a statewide board. The university includes six colleges, business, nursing, education, applied science and technology, arts and sciences, and music. CSU has publicly stated that its mission is undergraduate education. The enrollment of the institution is 10,000 undergraduate students. Graduate student enrollment is 1200 across master's degree programs in business, education, nursing, and music. CSU serves a diverse student population from across the region. Staying true to its mission, CSU has begun to evaluate ways of strengthening the undergraduate academic experience.

Dr. Durham, Dean for Undergraduate Education, has been asked by the provost, Dr. Pepper, to chair a committee that would develop a general education program for CSU. The idea was endorsed by President Harvey and his administrative council where the vice president of student affairs, Dr. Indyana, announced that she would like to also serve on the committee. She believed her division could offer assistance in improving the undergraduate educational experience at CSU. Although not all of the members of the administrative council understood how student "services" could enhance the academic experiences of students, Dr. Harvey agreed to appoint Dr. Indyana to the committee.

Dr. Pepper assembled the general education committee with

faculty from across the colleges: four from the College of Arts and Science (CAS), one from the College of Music, one from the College of Applied Science and Technology, one from the College of Nursing, one from the College of Education, and one from the College of Business. Communication about the direction of the general education program was difficult; initially faculty could only discuss the general education curriculum from their own professional perspective. The committee's charge was to develop a program that would provide a common foundation for the baccalaureate degree. The foundation of the program needed to be liberal in its view of knowledge, have a focus on the development of the person, interdisciplinary in its educational approach, and global in its educational perspective. The general education program should develop skills and content knowledge from basic through higher levels of intellectual development. The common foundation was to be integrated and interactive with all majors, emphasizing the coherence of knowledge and learning across all areas and levels of study while retaining a commitment to the distinctive character of the general education program (within 39 credit hours).

The committee began by discussing courses that should be included in the 39 credit hours:

Professor Murphy (philosophy) "Students need to read things that will broaden their minds intellectually. I recommend that first year students use a book on advanced philosophy that gives them an idea of the expectations of graduate programs."

Associate Professor Rosales (women's studies) "Students need to understand the issues surrounding women's oppression in the world that none of us learned in our own undergraduate education."

Professor James (Education) "I can offer a perspective on issues we face with students who come with secondary educations that are often lacking."

Associate Professor Holmen (Business) "The general education program must include technical skill development for students."

Professor Hamrick (Computer Systems) "The entire general education program should include the latest in high technology for the well being of future generations of students."

Professor Needles (Nursing) "Why can't they just leave us to provide the courses that the students need for their professions."

Distinguished Professor Mbilizi (Music) "A general education must expose students to the importance of music and art across the centuries."

Assistant Professors Terry and Brady (English and Mathematics) both wonder why they have to cooperate with non arts and sciences faculty to create a general education program.

As the meeting goes on, Dr. Indyana becomes more frustrated with the direction the committee is taking. She realizes that she will need to be creative in order to help this faculty group improve undergraduate education.

This committee discussion is not unlike many such discussions on many campuses throughout the country. The chief student affairs officer must find a way to insinuate herself productively into this academic discussion even though the faculty members involved seem barely able to hear one another. In the sections that follow, we periodically revisit this case while examining the major components of our framework.

Input—Secondary Education, Home and Community Environments, and Student Characteristics— Makes a Difference in Students' Learning.

Does background affect who goes to college, where one goes to college, and how well one performs in college? Sociologists Pierre Bourdieu and Jean Claude Passeron are known for their work in social class, and cultural reproduction within educational systems. Bourdieu and Passeron (1990) view education as an important social and political force in the process of class reproduction. By appearing to be impartial and neutral "transmitters" of the benefits of a valued culture, educational institutions often inadvertently promote inequality in the name of fairness and objectivity. The Bourdieu and Passeron (1990) concept of cultural capital refers to the different sets of linguistic and cultural competencies that individuals "inherit" by way of the socioeconomic class of their families. In more specific terms, a child learns from his or her family sets of meanings, qualities of style, modes of thinking, and types of dispositions that are accorded a certain social value and status as a result of what the dominant class or classes label as most valued. These meanings, styles, modes, and dispositions can be called cultural capital. Secondary schools play a particularly important role in both legitimizing and reproducing the dominant culture.

At the level of higher education, colleges typically embody class interests and ideologies that capitalize on a kind of familiarity and set of skills that specific students have received by means of their family backgrounds and class relations (Bourdieu, 1977; Downey and Powell, 1993; Stage and Manning, 1992). A four-year college degree has often been referred to as a ticket into the American middle class (Bowles and Gintis, 1976). Upward mobility in American society is defined by changes in occupational status and income and is inextricably linked to postsecondary education in modern American society (Pascarella and Terenzini, 1991).

Because we are sincere in our efforts to create maximum learning environments, we cannot afford to ignore the effects of family background and status experiences; more time in understanding students' communities, concerns, and problems is warranted. How are we to motivate and inspire if we do not know our students and their rationale for seeking enrollment? This question may seem rather trivial; however, we assume that the purpose of attending a post secondary institution is educational or vocational. If students were asked why they come to college, we can expect such responses as, 'I had nothing better to do," "My parents wanted me to come," "For a better way of life," "To find a job," and "for the love of knowledge" (Stage, 1989, p. 390). These motivations are explicitly tied to the cultural capital students bring with them to college. And, whatever the reasons, student affairs professionals and faculty must work with students who are described in the literature as lonely, isolated, poorly guided, unequipped intellectually, unmotivated, and passive in their quest for learning. Students' differing motivations add complexity to an already diverse student population. Let us return to Central State University:

The University's general education committee addresses one of their first tasks, to design a program with a common foundation for students who seek degrees. Dr. Indyana suggests to Dr. Durham that the committee might begin by examining the students themselves and looking at how they might have changed. She reminds the committee that twenty years ago the school accepted only students in the top 30% of their graduating classes. In recent years they have dipped slightly below the top 50% in order to maintain enrollments. As a result many students are first generation college attendees. Additionally, the committee sees more returning and part time students and, in the past decade, have seen increasing num-

bers of ethnic minority students matriculate. The committee launch-
es into a discussion of various "deficits" in the preparation of their
students. Many have never read an original Shakespeare play. Most
lack basic algebra skills. Many declared science majors have no
understanding of the phrase "scientific method."

After lengthy discussion, Dr. Durham gets the group to grudg-
ingly admit that, given the competitive climate for students, the
Admissions Office is probably recruiting the best students it can.
Dr. Indyana volunteers to bring more detailed information about
students to the next meeting, information in addition to the general admissions numbers, as well as some case studies that demonstrate the variety of students and their preparation for college. Next
time, she thinks to herself, I will broach the matter of learning
styles and students' motivations and decides to bring the data she
has on that as well.

The committee's next task will be to create a curriculum with a
foundation for all students that is liberal while integrating knowledge and providing interaction between and among all majors, emphasizing the coherence of knowledge and learning across all areas
and levels of study while retaining a commitment to developing the
students toward life long learning. One might idealistically envision
the faculty making fewer assumptions about knowledge levels of students in their classes and begin to reexamine some of their assumptions in the first days of class. An English professor might broaden
the expectation that a student had read Shakespeare to the expectation that the student had read and/or had written or participated in
writing a play. Developmental classes and special skills development
activities might be used to take care of other perceived "deficits."
At the very least, as a result of this experience, as committee members report back to their departments, faculty develop a better understanding of their students.

As the faculty committee begins to discuss what courses students
should have in common, one can imagine disagreements that align
themselves along the disciplines represented by the various professors. Because there are so many different departments in various
locations, faculty rarely interact with each other. As student affairs
professionals or educators, we enter the conversation to guide faculty attention toward discussion focusing on who their students are and
the assets they bring to college.

The Process—Quality of Effort, College Environment, and Other Environments—Influences Student Learning

We have shown that student affairs professionals have access to information that faculty can benefit from in designing more inviting and meaningful learning experiences inside classrooms. Faculty and student affairs professionals can work together to inform each other in ways that can facilitate student learning. All too often, the objectives of programs, services, and classes are based on assumptions and traditions rather than facts. A campus that is committed to learning considers expanding boundaries and plans in a wholistic manner.

Today's students require more of faculty and student affairs professionals because of diversity in students' socioeconomic status, intellectual abilities, cultures, and ages. New and creative ways making the campus a welcoming environment for students we have actively recruited is indeed a challenge (Stage and Manning, 1992). Students from various backgrounds come together for a common goal, to learn. While learning, students also seek familiarity in other students, in college officials and faculty, and in the places and things they encounter (Stage and Manning, 1992). Faculty and student affairs professionals can work together to create "zones of familiarity" for students.

In a study using the College Student Experience Questionnaire (CSEQ), White students at small private liberal arts institutions described high level of educational gains but a low level of involvement in contrast to Black students who revealed the opposite (Watson, 1994; Watson and Kuh, 1996). One reason for this finding might be that White students had more options to become involved in activities in the local community (factors the CSEQ does not measure); hence, they spent less time on the college campus. The Black students were more involved on the college campus but reported significantly lower educational gains, implying that the college activities that were measured were unrelated to the educational gains of Black students at this particular institution. Additionally, the results suggest that assumptions we make based on experiences with populations of largely white students may need to be adjusted for more diverse groups of students.

As educators we are prompted to ask questions: "what kinds of activities are students engaged in off campus that would increase their educational gains?"; "what are Black students engaged in on campus that is not increasing their educational gains?" What is it about differences that exist between and among our students that affect their motivation, learning, involvement, and educational gains? As the student population continues to evolve, we must be equally concerned with the same basic questions for international students, returning students, and older students. In short, how do we provide adequate services and programs to challenge and support these groups of students to become involved in meaningful activities to maximize their learning and development? Additionally, we must remember that an institution of higher education should be a place where people grow through meaningful relationships that are developed among faculty, administrators, staff, and students for their mutual benefit. How can we assist students in these important ventures?

The person-environment theories are a major conceptual tool used by educators and practitioners to describe students' behavior and to understand how students adapt in the college environment (Chapman *and* Pascarella, 1983; Thompson and Fretz, 1991). Person-environment theories provide avenues for thinking about how the college environment affects student involvement, change, and development. Pervin (1968) hypothesized that an ideal environment for any given individual is one in which the congruence of individual and environment is not exact. The ideal environment would hold a predominance of individuals with many congruent characteristics but also present opportunities for change and personal growth. However, challenge without support to learn and develop can result in dissatisfaction and, in the campus setting, withdrawal.

Withdrawal from the institution is a major concern for educators, and Tinto's (1975) theory of retention hypothesizes that attrition results from sociopsychological interaction between a student and the educational environment. Each student brings to the college campus various factors, background, personal attributes, and experiences, and these factors influence college performance, initial goals and institutional commitment (some of these individual attributes are discussed in Chapter 2). Such factors and institutional environments lead to differences in integration into the academic and social systems of the institution. Bean's (1980) model of student attrition describes prematriculation characteristics of students that are expected to influence how the student interacts with the environment and intent to dropout or not.

Bean (1980) also looks at external factors or "non-intellectual" factors that play a major role in student persistence. Pascarella's general model for assessing change also emphasizes the student's background characteristics, interactions with major socializing agents, and the quality of student's effort (Pascarella and Terenzini, 1991). For most of the persistence models, the focus is primarily on the environments within the boundaries of the institution. However, the effects of external environments on student learning are also powerful. Student experiences working or volunteering in the community can motivate them when they see the applicability of theories. "Service learning" and its effect on the total educational experience is the topic of a later chapter.

The SLI supports the notion of collaborative efforts of all campus and community agents working together to integrate the curriculum and co-curriculum. The SLI suggests that enhancement of student learning is not only defined by faculty, but by those environments and conditions that encourage, inspire, and motivate students to actively participate in their educational pursuits. Collaboration between student affairs units and families, communities, and secondary schools has recently begun to draw more attention for creating ideal learning environments for college students (Lempert, 1996; Stage, 1996). By expanding our traditional boundaries to include secondary schools, business, and community, we can begin to better understand our students and their needs before they arrive on the college campus (Harper and Harston, 1996; Terrell and Watson, 1996; Weidman, 1989). Returning once again to our curriculum committee, we see some new ways of approaching old problems:

Dr. Indyana comes to the next meeting armed with data. Throughout her presentation she prompts committee members to speculate about the differences between students of 20 years ago (for whom the current curriculum was designed) and today's students. From there she moves to a brief presentation on learning styles, discussing typical faculty styles as well as differences in styles for students of various ethnic groups. In the discussion that ensues Professors James and Terry describe activities in their own classes that are designed to vary learning tasks and student demonstrations of their learning. A heated discussion results in Professors Murphy and Hamrick wondering whether we will next be advocating an individual lesson plan for each student in the classroom. Some around the table allow as how such innovation might be easy to implement in some practical courses like education or nursing but those ideas won't really help in courses where the students' job is to learn. Indyana makes a mental note to catch the student reporter for the Central State Issues to give her some more detail on the topic. The committee decides they would like to hear more from faculty who are actually trying some of these innovations especially those related to incorporating students' cultural backgrounds and community experiences in their classes. After two hours Durham calls the end of the meeting. Later Indyana catches Durham and suggests that Professor Rhoads' service learning project in criminal justice be one of the featured classes.

Learning and Development Benefit the Individual, Society and Future Generations

Pascarella and Terenzini (1991), in their review of 2,600 research studies, concluded that students make gains in cognitive skills, general verbal skills, general quantitative skills, and substantial advances in knowledge of a specific subject matter related to their field of study. The intellectual changes that occur from freshmen-to-senior year include: an improved ability to reason abstractly; the ability to solve problems or puzzles within a scientific paradigm; an enhanced skill in using reason and evidence to address issues and problems; and development as effective speakers and writers (Bowen, 1977; Pascarella and Terenzini, 1991).

In addition, students seem to move toward greater self-understanding, self-definition, personal commitment, and refinement of ego functioning as they move from their first year to senior status. The psychosocial changes experienced during college permeate throughout the students' lives in the manner in which they interact with other people and other aspects of their external world. Students show modest gains in personal adjustment, sense of psychological well-being, personal development, maturity, and tolerance of other people and ideas. "As the students become better learners, they also appear to become increasingly independent of parents, gain in their sense that they are in control of their world and what happens to them, and become somewhat more mature in their interpersonal relations, both in general and in their intimate relations with others, whether of the same or opposite sex" (Pascarella and Terenzini, 1991, p. 562).

Evidence connecting college experiences with the long-term gains and "quality of life indexes" is not very strong. When holding economic resources constant, many quality of life differences still exist (Pascarella and Terenzini, 1991). For example, the college experience has a moderate affect on one's health status, family size, consumer behavior, savings and investment, marital satisfaction, and life satisfaction index; it has a weak affect on marital stability, nurturance of children, cultured leisure, and job satisfaction (Pascarella and Terenzini, 1991). Much evidence suggests that having college-educated parents positively affects the socioeconomic achievement of sons and daughters and the educational attainment of children.

Yet, Pascarella and Terenzini acknowledge that having college-educated parents may enhance the cognitive development of young children through the indirect route of the home environment. As Bourdieu and Passeron (1990) discussed earlier, college-educated parents and particularly mothers pass on benefits to their children through time spent on developmental activities such as reading and teaching.

> The long-term trend of these intergenerational legacies appears to be not only toward greater socioeconomic security and well being but also toward greater cognitive growth and openness, tolerance, and concern for human rights and liberties. To a greater degree, the long-term effects of college on attitudes and values may also involve an intergenerational effect; the attitudes and values that students develop at least partially as a consequence of their college experience are passed on to their children. (Pascarella and Terenzini, 1991. p. 586)

Again we revisit the curriculum committee:

> By the third meeting Indyana feels that much of her work has been completed. She has used her leadership and influence to set the committee in a direction that broadens and informs their view of students as they consider the outcomes that they desire, and then begin to design the curriculum. She was successful in involving innovative faculty leaders to demonstrate their own ideas and to provide examples for other faculty rather than telling the faculty what she thought they ought to be doing. A final charge to the committee was to develop a plan to ensure that the goals and objectives of the curriculum are met. She knows that as they move toward the end of the year and the committee turns its attention toward evaluation and assessment, her leadership skills will be critical to the committee work. For now, she welcomes participation as one of the ten committee members developing a plan to renew Central State University.

Conclusions and Recommendations

The framework presented in this chapter on student learning, involvement, and educational gains is designed to encourage us to think more broadly about our students when planning programs, enhancing services, and designing the co-curriculum. With the shortage of funds and demands on our time, it is often easy to rekindle last year's programs for this year's students. In fact, in times of reduced resources, keeping up with day to day operations can become overwhelming. Often little time exists to plan a program to stimulate growth for the diverse student population we encounter on our campuses. The diversity of our student body necessitates a wholistic understanding of students in order to assist them in their learning. How often do we really think about strategically planning our efforts to consider where a student is from and how that background might influence his or her participation in college experiences? Are we proactive in our efforts to identify students who may need support to become successful graduates? And, do we inform and identify those people who could and should get involved to support us in our efforts?

By using Watson's (1994, 1996) conceptual framework on learning, involvement, and gains, one may begin to focus more closely on the relationships among input, process, and output for the purpose of educational decision making regarding services and programming for students (Figure 1). A number of factors including student characteristics, college environment, and quality of effort influence students' educational gains. When employing the conceptual framework, here are some suggestions:

- Look at the programs that are currently in place. Ask such questions as: What are the true purposes of the program; and for whom were they designed? Consider the three areas of Watson's framework to evaluate and update programs to services. Assessment and feedback (Figure 1) of the "input, process, and output" factors should be conducted as regularly as possible due to the changing nature of students and society.

- In creating new programs, eliminate duplication of resources. Conduct research to see if outside organizations have similar programs that may be of help before instituting a new program. Ask such questions as: Will this program meet the needs of students? Have I considered those background characteristics that should be considered to enhance learning? What are the expected outcomes of the program and how will they be measured? How will feedback or assessment be reported for improvements or informational purposes?

- Encourage the creation of advisory or project teams, task forces, and committees that include students, faculty and administrators from across disciplines, and the external community. Ensure strong support for collaboration with various groups.

- Plan to provide additional management training and recruitment support as needed to ensure the availability of qualified professionals who can discuss the nature of student learning and development with various groups in both the external and internal environments.

Because we are educators, it is imperative that we involve ourselves in the total education of students including: teaching students how to be better learners; how to think critically in order to solve complex problems; and how to transfer skills from one situation to another. Now is the time for educators to make a commitment that focuses on building a community to maximize student learning. If we believe it is our responsibility as student affairs professionals to challenge and support students to their fullest potential, we should incorporate in our practices a wholistic approach to our work. Such an approach will require us to move out of our comfort zones and also challenge and support other professionals and colleagues across the university community to think of their work in different ways in order to enhance students' educational outcomes.

References

American College Personnel Association (ACPA). (1994). *The student learning imperative: Implications for student affairs.* Washington, DC: Author.

Astin, A. W. (1984). Student involvement: A developmental theory for higher education. *Journal of College Student Development, 26,* 297–308.

Bean, J. (1980). Dropout and turnover: The synthesis and test of a causal model of student attrition. *Research in Higher Education, 12,* 155–187.

Bourdieu, P. (1977). The cultural transmission of social inequality. *Harvard Educational Review, 47,* 545–555.

Bourdieu, P., and Passeron, J. (1990). *Reproduction in education, society and culture.* Beverly Hills: Sage.

Bowen, H. (1977). *Investment in learning: The individual and social values of American higher education.* San Francisco: Jossey-Bass.

Bowles, S., and Gintis, H. (1976). *Schooling in capitalist America.* New York: Basic Books.

Chapman, D., and Pascarella, E. (1983). Predictors of academic and social integration of college students. *Research in Higher Education, 19* 295–322.

Domjan, M. (1993). *The principles of learning and behavior.* Pacific Grove, CA: Brooks/Cole.

Downey, D. B. (1994). Understanding academic achievement among children in stephouseholds: The role of parental resources, sex of stepparent, and sex of child. *Social Forces, 73*(3), 875–894.

Downey, D.B. and Powell, B. (1993). Do children in singleparent households fare better living with samesex parents? *Journal of Marriage and the Family, 55,* 55–71.

Feldman, K., and Newcomb, T. (1969). *The impact of college on students.* San Francisco: Jossey-Bass.

Harper, J., and Harston, A. (1996). K16 Collaboration: University professionals of Illinois and the Chicago teacher union. *Universities 21,* 2, 47.

Lempert, D. H. (1996).*Escape from the ivory tower: Student adventures in democratic experiential education.* San Francisco: Jossey-Bass.

National Association of Student Personnel Administrators (NASPA). (1987). A perspective on student affairs: A statement issued on the 50th anniversary of The Student Personnel Point of View. Washington, DC: Author.

Pace, C. R. (1984). *Measuring the quality of college students experiences.* University of California, Los Angeles: Higher Education Research Institute.

Pace, C. R. (1988). *CSEQ: Test manual & norms.* University of California, Los Angeles: Center for the study of evaluation.

Pascarella, E., and Terenzini, P. (1991). *How college affects students.* San Francisco: JosseyBass.

Pervin, L. A. (1968). Performance and satisfaction as a function of individualenvironment fit. *Psychological Bulletin, 69,* 565–8.

Stage, F. K. (1989). Motivation, academic and social integration, and the early dropout. *American Educational Research Journal,* 26,

Stage, F. K. (1996). Setting the context: Psychological theories of learning. *Journal of College Student Development,* 37(2), 227–235.

Stage, F., and Manning, K. (1992). *Enhancing the multicultural campus environment: A cultural brokering approach.* New Directions for Student Affairs, No. 60, 110. San Francisco: Jossey-Bass.

Terrell, M. and Watson, L. (1996). Collaborative Partnerships for a Diverse Campus Community. *Journal of College Student Development, 37,* 249253.

Tinto, V. (1975). Dropouts from higher education: A theoretical synthesis of recent research. *Review of Education Research,* 45, 89–125.

Thompson, C., and Fretz, B. (1991). Predicting the adjustment of black students at predominantly white institutions. *Journal of higher education, 62,* 437–450.

Watson, L. W. (1994). *An analysis of Black and White students' perceptions, involvement, and educational gains in private historically Black and White liberal arts institutions.* Unpublished doctoral dissertation, Indiana University, Bloomington, IN.

Watson, L. W. (1996). A collaborative approach to student learning: A model for administrators in higher education. *Planning and Changing: An Educational Leeadership and Policy Journal.*

Watson, L. W. and Kuh, G. (1996). The influence of dominant race environments on student involvement, perceptions, and educational gains: A look at historically black and predominantly white liberal arts institutions. *Journal of College Student Development,* 37, 415–424.

Weidman, J. (1989). Undergraduate socialization: A conceptual approach. In J. Smart (ed.), *Higher education: Handbook of theory and research.* New York: Agathon.

2

Theories of Learning for College Students

Frances K. Stage
Patricia Muller

This chapter focuses on an important element of Watson's (1996) model described in Chapter 1, the personal characteristics of students related to learning. As described earlier, students come to the campus shaped by their cultural capital and various educational histories that influence how they experience the educational process. Efforts by faculty and student affairs professionals within the educational process can influence these elements in positive or negative directions. By focusing on theories related to learning, we can more fully describe our own efforts as well as design new endeavors that go hand in hand with academic programs on our campuses.

This chapter begins with a summary of the usefulness of theory including currently used cognitive development theories. Next is a brief overview of psychological theories of learning. Theories that hold particular relevance to learning within aspects of student affairs that relate to academic success are described—self-efficacy, constructivist learning theories, multiple intelligences and learning styles, and conscientization. Examples and suggestions for application to student affairs work are discussed. Finally, the context is set for discussions in the remaining chapters.

Usefulness of Theory

Since the late 1980s the usefulness of psychological development theories on college campuses has gone largely unquestioned. Cognitive development theories in particular stem from the discipline of psychology and have proven especially useful in gauging students' growth and decision making. Cognitive theorists believe that cognitive conflict with an optimal amount of dissonance (conflict within a supportive environment) leads to development.

As student affairs professionals many of us are familiar with cognitive development theories that portray development as a series of stepwise progressions focusing on "how we think" and not "what we think." For example, Perry's (1981) theory of intellectual and cognitive development has been widely used to better understand college student development. This theory traces students' evolution in thinking about the nature of knowledge, truth and values through a scheme consisting of three general levels—dualism, relativism, and commitment. Perry describes the process by which students move from a simplistic, categorical view of the world that is viewed through absolute terms (dualism), to a more contextual view of the world that acknowledges a multiplicity of viewpoints (relativism), to the highest level of development characterized by a clarification of values and personal commitments (commitment in relativism).

Other cognitive development theories focusing on moral reasoning (Kohlberg, 1981; Gilligan, 1982) are also widely used on college campuses. According to the Kohlberg, each stage of moral reasoning reflects the students' changing basis for deciding what is the "just" or "fair" way to resolve a moral dilemma. For the student at preconventional levels, the personal consequences of an act or decision distinguish right from wrong. At conventional levels of development, laws, conventions and responsibilities defined by a social system form the basis for justifying decisions. Finally, at postconventional levels, Kohlberg's highest levels, abstract moral principals such as human rights, social welfare and universal ethical principles form the basis of the individual's morality.

Gilligan (1982) developed an alternative view of moral development that was more inclusive of women's decision making than Kohlberg's study that was originally based on adolescent men. Gilligan's theory, based predominantly on women's experiences, contends that for some people the balance between relationships and responsibilities plays a more prominent role than social justice in moral decision-making. Other cognitive development theories include Kitchener and King's (1990) reflective judgement theory, and Belenky, Clinchy, Goldberger and Tarule's (1986) model of epistemological development, based on in-depth interviews with 135 women.

As student affairs professionals many of us have become accustomed to using cognitive development theories. These developmental theories allow us to describe observed differences between students. As an academic advisor, I can more readily recognize a dualistic student's desire to be given firm advice and provide the student with a more limited set of choices for an elective based on my knowledge of his strengths and previous selections. As a faculty advisor of a student on a judicial board I listen to a student judge's struggles with relativism then ask her to consider those whose rights are violated when others are given complete freedom of expression.

Employing theory has proven useful to us for several reasons:

1. Theory provides a framework with which to connect our experiences and observations about college students;

2. Through oral and written language, theory allows us to communicate with others and connect our experiences with theirs; and

3. Theory guides our experiments to observe whether our theories work. We can see theory in action at the workshops and sessions of our national conferences as well as in the literature of our profession.

In those contexts we are able to take advantage of the work of theorists and researchers who have preceded us as well as inform and influence those who will follow. In this chapter we suggest an expansion of our uses of psychological theory to those focusing specifically on learning.

We have another compelling reason to incorporate psychological learning theories in our efforts to enhance student learning on campus as well. In our various academic worlds verbal communication is valued and information is currency. Theory provides us with the language and the currency that connects us to academic research that many of our colleagues understand and expect in the college setting. When we can support our decisions and suggestions with research, often more people will listen. Utilizing theory to improve our practice enables us to make an intellectual connection that helps administrators, academics, and graduate students understand us and the importance of our relationships to student learning (Stage, 1996; Stage, Muller, Kinzie and Simmons, 1998).

Theories of Learning

A behaviorist view of humans and their interactions with the world dominated psychological theories during the first part of this century. B. F. Skinner (1953, 1968), one well-known theorist, believed the goal of psychology was to predict and control behavior. Following the mainstream social science tradition of the scientific method, learning was often studied within carefully controlled experimental settings that were frequently far removed from the complex realities of actual learning. The influence of behaviorist theory is still evident today in teaching and learning on the college campus.

Psychological theorists have taken a more cognitive approach to learning during the last part of this century. The discipline of educational psychology has focused heavily on cognitive functioning and on how people process, organize, and retrieve information. Context has taken on increased significance within these cognitive frameworks. Much of college student learning often occurs embedded within a classroom context. Translation of that learning into job related activities and decision-making is usually difficult within the classroom context (Glover, Ronning, and Bruning, 1990). Additionally, many psychologists believe that "knowledge in human memory seems to be 'stored' in contextual fashion" (Glover, Ronning, and Bruning, 1990, p. 23). Classroom activities that represent the complexity of job situations and decision-making in the "real world" do not frequently exist. As student affairs professionals we can contribute extensively to the learning process through activities structured outside the classroom. For example, leadership opportunities, judicial activities, and tutoring rendered within the framework of student affairs can provide contexts within which students can interpret their classroom learning experiences. Learning processes developed in coordination with the curriculum, such as service learning experiences, can also complement and suplement the learning process. For each of the theories described in this chapter, we provide examples of the ways that a student affairs related activity or experience might add to the learning process.

Traditionally, the field of student affairs has emphasized the student development and learning that takes place outside the classroom.

In more recent years the term extra-curricular has frequently been replaced with "co-curricular" to stress that out-of-class learning occurs alongside the formal academic curriculum, and is integral to the educational process. However, student affairs professionals often describe these out-of-classroom activities as distinctly separate from the formal academic classroom. Here we use these learning theories to identify particular "inputs" that are characteristic of students as discussed in chapter one. Then we seek to modify the "process" that leads to learning. As members of a changing student affairs profession, part of our role might be described as reinterpreting the contexts within which college learning takes place by more directly linking the learning activities that occur outside the classroom with the learning that occurs within a classroom context. As *context setters* student affairs professionals working with faculty, students, and others can help provide experiences that give structure and meaning to classroom learning for college students.

The remainder of this chapter describes several theories, some psychological, that hold particular relevance for increasing student affairs professionals' capacity to enhance student learning. Although limiting the selection of theories to include was difficult, we chose several that seem related in their attempts to describe learning. The description of theories is by no means intended to be exhaustive, and many learning theories still need to be examined regarding their relevance to student affairs. As with student development theories, overlap and similarities exist that should be comforting to us as various scholars attempt to describe the phenomenon of human learning (Stage, 1991). These overlapping observations by diverse scholars serve to highlight aspects of learning that are pervasive and important. It is our hope that readers find these theories (as well as their overlapping principles) useful as they set the context for learning on their own college campuses.

Perceived Self-efficacy

The importance of perceived self-efficacy in learning is described in-depth by Bandura (1986; 1993; 1994; 1997). He claims that no mechanism of personal agency is "more central or pervasive than people's [self-efficacy] beliefs" (Bandura, 1993, p. 118). Self-efficacy is defined as individuals' beliefs about their capabilities to exercise control over their own levels of functioning and to exert influence over events that affect their lives (Bandura, 1994). Self-efficacy beliefs influence an individual's feelings, thinking, motivations, and behaviors.

Bandura and his colleagues demonstrated that both the self-efficacy beliefs of students and the collective beliefs of teachers (in their instructional efficacy) contributed significantly to levels of academic achievement in school settings (Bandura, 1993). Self-efficacy beliefs also produced achievement effects through motivational processes, either enhancing or decreasing motivation.

Through cognitive, motivational, and affective and selection processes (see Bandura, 1993), self-efficacy beliefs produce effects on academic achievement. Given the focus of this chapter on cognitive learning theories, we will primarily focus on the cognitive processes. For the college student, prior conceptions of ability (often based on experiences in previous educational settings), social comparisons (comparative evaluations within classes, living environments, and co-curricular contexts), framing of feedback (the social evaluation of achieved progress or shortfalls), and perceived controllability (locus of control) all combine for the development of self-efficacy. Therefore, building a sense of self-efficacy that promotes learning for college students involves constructing learning environments that construe ability as an acquirable skill, de-emphasize competitive social comparisons and highlight self-comparison of progress and personal accomplishment, and reinforce students' ability to exercise some control of their learning environment.

Since most human motivation is cognitively generated, beliefs of self-efficacy also play a critical role in student motivation and subsequent behaviors (Bandura, 1993). Positive expectations regarding outcomes of behavior and the value of those outcomes as well as explicit challenging goals enhance and sustain motivation. These goals guide students' behaviors and create incentives to persist until these goals are fulfilled. People set challenging goals for themselves and thereby create a state of disequilibrium, which they then reduce by accomplishing the goals. College students constantly set goals, fail or succeed, readjust the goals, and begin the cycle again in a dynamic and continual process of self regulation, adjustment, and re-evaluation.

Affective processes form an emotional component of self-efficacy. Students' beliefs in their own capabilities affect the amount of stress and depression they experience in difficult academic or social situations. This can be seen, for example, in a student with minimal coping efficacy whose disturbing thought patterns lead to test anxiety, interfering with the student's ability to perform.

Self-efficacy also contributes to the type of social reality students construct for themselves through selection processes. Self-efficacy beliefs shape students' lives through their influence on selection of activities, environments, and careers. Choices of educational opportunities and social networks are also influenced by students' perceived self-efficacy. In focusing specifically on the transition from adolescence to adulthood, Bandura (in press) describes the particular importance of structured transitions such as those provided within the context of colleges and universities.

Bandura's (1993) work on self-efficacy forms an important basis for consideration of learning on the college campus. The campus community can provide the context within which a student who does not initially excel in the formal classroom acquires skills and abilities that are useful and valued in the real life arena. Through the development of capabilities, and through the positive framing of performance feedback on achieved progress, students' beliefs about themselves become increasingly positive. In turn, their motivation to perform and, ultimately, their actual performance are enhanced. With success, and feedback that continues to underscore personal capabilities, beliefs about self-efficacy become even more positive. The student's motivation and performance proceeds in a continual reciprocal relationship.

Self-efficacy is highly domain specific (Pressley and McCormick, 1995), and high self-efficacy in one domain is not necessarily correlated with the level of self-efficacy in a different domain. For example, a college student might have high self-efficacy with respect to math and science, but low self-efficacy with regard to writing or leadership skills. These beliefs about personal efficacy play a key role in a student's choice of career and major. They can be restrictive, for example, when a college student with a low sense of efficacy in mathematics chooses a major because it does not have a mathematics requirement. Self-efficacy beliefs can likewise be enabling for a student who has positive beliefs about his or her own ability to learn difficult material (Bandura, 1997). Students who have a low sense of efficacy in a given domain will shy away from a difficult task, whereas students with a positive sense of self-efficacy are more likely to take risks and attempt challenging tasks. As students move through college and into adulthood, their sense of self-efficacy is likely to crystallize. Challenging tasks that are met successfully will likely increase self-efficacy in ways that promote future attempts at challenging tasks. Conversely, tasks that are too challenging can erode an individual's sense of efficacy and thwart ambition.

Mastery experiences, vicarious experiences, social persuasion, and somatic and emotional states further influence the development of students' beliefs about efficacy (Bandura, 1994). Student affairs professionals can structure learning contexts that allow students to engage successfully in activities that capitalize on these four main sources of influence on self-efficacy. Self-efficacy can be positively influenced through activities that provide opportunities to experience mastery, watch others like themselves succeed and thus experience success vicariously, and be persuaded by their peers to participate in challenging activities. These learning contexts will assist students in developing positive, less stressful reactions to challenges.

For example, an academic advisor works with Kandace, an African American student who is having academic difficulty. During their advising session, he asks Kandace about her high school experiences and learns that she was president of a service club and very involved in campus activities, although she has not made such connections at college. The advisor suggests that for next semester Kandace enroll in a journalism class with a service learning component and arranges for a meeting with another African American advisee who is involved in a campus service fraternity. If all goes well, these activities can help provide Kandace with more of the kinds of successes, vicarious experiences, and positive social reinforcement that can lead to a more successful college experience.

As student affairs professionals, the *Student Learning Imperative* (American College Personnel Association, 1994) encourages us to capitalize on students' beliefs in their self-efficacy by developing learning activities both related to and outside of regular college classroom activities. Part of our role in student affairs is to help students find contexts in which they can develop their self-efficacy by capitalizing on their diverse talents and ways of learning (Chickering and Gamson, 1987).

Constructivist Theories of Learning

The discussion of constructivist theories of learning typically occurs within the context of elementary and secondary mathematics and science classrooms. Yet the principles of constructivist learning are logical and easily extend to other contexts. Constructivism is based upon the basic tenet that knowledge is not merely transmitted from one person to another, but results from an individual's knowledge-construction process wherein knowledge is actively learned and sub-jectively known. Constructivists emphasize the importance of learn-ing within the context of reality and stress the importance of physical experiences that encourage learners to attempt to understand and in-terpret phenomena for themselves. At the extreme, a constructivist believes that given sufficient equipment and time, accompanied by minimal guidance in a laboratory, a student would discover all he or she needed to know about, for example, chemistry.

Social constructivism, a modification of constructivist theory, has also been used to describe the learning process, particularly within the contexts of mathematics and science. Driver, Asoko, Leach, Moritmer, and Scott (1994) describe the ways in which the learner, in conjunction with discovery, is "initiated into scientific ways of knowing" (p. 6). As the young scientist makes "discoveries" the teach-er helps the student place his or her discoveries within the frame-work of science as described by current scientists. Since the "objects of science are not the phenomena of nature, but the constructs that are advanced by the scientific community to interpret nature" (p. 5), these constructs (e.g., rates of chemical reactions, atoms, genes and chromosomes) are unlikely to be discovered by individuals through observation alone. Science educators help their learners mediate sci-entific knowledge and help them make personal sense of the ways in which knowledge claims are generated and validated rather than sim-ply leaving learners on their own to organize their own individual sense-makings about the natural world (Driver et al, 1994). Learning and understanding then occur when individuals engage socially in dialogue and activities around shared problems or tasks, with knowl-edge-construction being facilitated by teachers' enculturation of stu-dents into discourses. The teacher serves as mediator and guide in the knowledge-construction process.

Many campus learning situations rely on a constructivist approach to learning. For example, resident assistant positions often engage students in dialogue and activities around "real life" problems and tasks such as crisis management, interpersonal skills, leadership skills, conflict resolution, team work, and counseling. The knowledge-con-struction process is supported by a supervisor or advisor who pro-vides intellectual links between theory and practice. Students also actively engage in knowledge-construction and better understand and interpret constructs from the classroom through involvement in stu-dent organization leadership positions, campus judicial boards, stu-dent government, volunteer organizations within the larger community, peer counseling or mentoring opportunities, or treasurer roles within organizations. Constructivist learning is operationalized through these physical experiences, combined with opportunities for individual reflection, and guided by student affairs professionals who engage students in dialogue and activities that facilitate intellectual links between these activities and interpretation in an academic context.

Similarly, many campuses have established service-learning programs that embrace many of the tenets of social constructivism. These approaches move beyond traditional internships, volunteerism, and community service efforts. Within these programs guidance and mentoring are provided to help students to make intellectual links with their practical learning. Ideally such links would be related to the students' academic coursework (Chapter 6 on service-learning). This "guided learning" is the trademark of service learning and does not take for granted that learning occurs merely because a student engages in activity.

On an individual basis, a student leader learning to manage an organization experiments with ways of working with various student groups. Over the course of several months or a year even a very gifted student leader might not be able to "discover" satisfactory patterns for dealing with group conflict. Using a social constructivist approach, an advisor could guide the student's discoveries by introducing basic readings in conflict management theory, personal communication styles, and group dynamics. Or ideally perhaps, the student has covered relevant materials in business and psychology classes and the discovery process is facilitated. The hallmark of social constructivist learning is the context or the reality of day-to-day life, not in place of other types of learning, but in close connection with them.

Multiple Intelligences and Learning Styles

Although not typically linked theoretically, multiple intelligences and learning styles hold similarities when viewed in terms of educators' expectations for their students. Both kinds of theories expand our view of the cognitive attributes of college students in a positive way.

Gardner's (1983) theory of multiple intelligences and subsequent research based on that theory (Gardner and Hatch, 1989) provides impetus for educators to expand notions of intelligence. Rather than simplistic notions of bicategorical verbal and mathematical intelligences, this body of work provides evidence of a multitude of intelligences traditionally ignored or undervalued in all educational settings. Gardner found at least seven forms of thinking (the seven intelligences) currently exhibited by individuals. The two intelligences traditionally emphasized and valued in American culture are logical-mathematical and linguistic.

Gardner adds to these intelligences five other intelligences that are traditionally undervalued in educational systems; the development of these intelligences is not stressed in most formal educational settings. Musical intelligence refers to abilities to produce and appreciate rhythm, pitch and timbre, and the appreciation of the forms of musical expressiveness. An individual with spatial intelligence has the capacity to accurately perceive the visual-spatial world, typified by navigators or sculptors. Bodily-kinesthetic intelligence is manifested in abilities to control body movements, well-developed fine motor skills, and adeptness at handling objects skillfully. Dancers and athletes are exemplars of this intelligence. Individuals with interpersonal intelligence, such as therapists and personnel directors, have the ability to respond effectively to the temperaments, motivations and desires of other persons. Intrapersonal skills are evident in persons with detailed, reflective self-knowledge. These persons are aware of their own strengths, weaknesses, desires and intelligences. Often, college students with learning disabilities display a high level of intrapersonal knowledge (Stage and Milne, 1996). These seven intelligences are not mutually exclusive categories, nor is there any necessary correlation between any two intelligences.

The challenge is for those of us who work with college students to find ways to value and enable all types of intelligence among the diversity of students who come to our campuses. As student affairs professionals we are in a unique position to foster the development of the intelligences that are traditionally underemphasized and undervalued in the classroom. For example, with the stimulus of a workshop based on multiple intelligences and help from a student affairs professional, an anthropology profesor redesigns his traditional term paper assignment. Through use of videos, the web, and museum collections, students may opt to conduct an in depth analysis and presentation of the music, dance, rituals, or other traditions of any of the cultures studied.

This notion of expansion of our expectations of students can be extended to discussions of learning styles (Anderson, 1988; Kolb, 1981; Rothschadl and Russell, 1992; Russell and Rothschadl, 1991). Perhaps Kolb's (1981) theory of learning styles is familiar to many readers of this volume, nevertheless, it is important enough to be described within the context of our expectations about student learning.

Kolb (1981) developed a typology describing learning styles of students in four categories: (a) convergers, (b) divergers, (c) assimilators, and (d) accommodators. Convergers are most comfortable with abstract concepts and active experimentation. They prefer practical applications of ideas, rarely exhibit emotion, and usually have specific interests. The diverger is most comfortable with concrete experience and reflective observation, often has a vivid imagination, and is able to view concrete situations from a variety of perspectives. The assimilator learns most effectively through abstract conceptualization and reflective observation. He or she excels in working with theoretical models and inductive reasoning. The accommodator learns best in a setting that allows for concrete experience and active experimentation; he or she prefers doing to thinking. Accommodators rely heavily on information from other people rather than theories, are very adaptable, and solve problems intuitively.

Kolb's and other related research has important implications for creation of a multicultural campus environment. Researchers have validated the presence of learning style differences in the college classroom (Russell and Rothschadl, 1991). Unsurprisingly, most faculty members tend to be assimilators. Abstract conceptualization and reflective observation, characteristic of assimilators, are assets for those who must "publish or perish." Those styles of thinking and learning heavily influence classroom assignments and evaluations on a typical college campus. Students who match the instructor's style are apt to feel most comfortable and be most successful in the college classroom. Those who don't may not have opportunities to use their own dominant learning style to advantage. Rothschadl and Russell (1992) provide suggestions for faculty who seek to broaden styles required by students in their classrooms.

Anderson (1988), in an elaboration of Kolb's theory, discussed the ways differences in minority and majority students' learning styles might affect success in college. Many majority students are comfortable with abstract theory and reflective observation (assimilators) that typifies college classroom learning. However, many minority students learn more easily with concrete examples and practical application, characteristic of divergers. Chapter one reminds us of the importance of taking into account students' divergent high school and family backgrounds when designing campus programs.

Anderson describes how, along the continuum of cognitive learning styles, certain racial/ethnic groups seem to cluster at one end or the other. The cognitive style of a group is strongly influenced by the cultural history of that group. Anderson discussed generalizations between non-western (American Indians, Mexican-Americans, African-Americans, Vietnamese-American, Puerto-Rican American, Chinese-American, Japanese-Americans and many Euro-American females) and western (Euro-American, primarily male, and minorities with a high degree of acculturation) cognitive styles. Non-western cultures tend to emphasize field-dependence. Individuals perform better on verbal tasks, value harmony and group cooperation, engage in relational and wholistic thinking, are socially oriented, and tend to incorporate the affective self into their cognitive evaluation of reality. Western cultures traditionally emphasize field-independence; individuals perform best on analytic tasks, seek to master and control nature, value individual competition and achievement, engage in more dualistic thinking, and limit affective expression. These cultural differences not only produce different learning styles, but also influence the more subtle aspects of perception and cognitive behavior.

Historically, school environments have valued and reinforced the cognitive learning style associated with Western culture while often misconstruing non-western styles as deficient (Anderson, 1988). Consequently, students of color frequently encounter difficulties when they attempt to adapt their styles to the abstract, field-independent, analytic styles of the academic classroom. This is especially true in mathematics and the hard sciences where teaching of the theory (in an abstract sense) precedes any practical application or direct, physical experience (e.g., laboratory experiments). A learning approach in which direct experience precedes, rather than follows, discussion of formal concepts and theories appears to better coincide with non-western cognitive styles. As student affairs professionals, we enhance the learning process of a broader range of students by providing concrete experiences drawn from everyday campus life that connect to students' more abstract classroom context.

Student leadership developed outside the classroom, for example, has long been assumed to represent a kind of personal development promoted by student affairs—but strong relationships exist with classroom studies of group processes; organizational mediation skills developed among students relate to psychology and sociology. Finally, a wealth of possibilities are inherent in service learning discussed in Chapter 6.

Frequently the student affairs administrator must serve as broker between a faculty member who may be rooted firmly in tradition, and diverse students. In chapter three we delve more deeply into the topic of approaches to and styles of learning for students of various cultural groups. By creating activities outside the classroom that better match students' learning styles, we can capitalize on the cultural and cognitive assets of all students.

Conscientization Theory

Although not traditionally, classified as a learning theory, Freire's pedagogy has important implications for learning. Freire's (1970) theory is typically viewed as a political process focusing on liberation and "conscientization." Conscientization is the process by which one moves from one level of consciousness to another, achieving a deepening awareness of one's socio-cultural reality. Freire is most popular in *informal* learning settings, making the principles of conscientization very applicable to the work of student affairs professionals outside the classroom.

Freire defines learning as an active process, and his theory opposes the "banking" concept of learning in which the learner passively accepts "deposits" of information. Conscientization involves a process that begins with the learner's ideas, words and life situation. The theory emphasizes learning as a dialogical action between learners and educators, with the educator's role as a coordinator or co-investigator helping the learners become aware of their life situations.

Conscientization consists of four levels. The lowest level of consciousness, intransitive consciousness, is characterized by the learner's preoccupation with meeting the most elementary needs, and a limited self-awareness of one's socio-cultural situation. Semi-intransitivity or magical consciousness, the second level, is characterized by "cultures of silence" and an acceptance of one's socio-cultural situation as a "given." Learners at this level view life as beyond their control (external locus of control), and these persons may exhibit signs of self-deprecation and low levels of self-efficacy. The third level of consciousness is naive, semi-transitive, or popular consciousness. At this level, the learner begins to seriously question his or her socio-cultural situation, albeit at a primitive level, and begins to develop a stronger locus of control. The highest level of consciousness is critical consciousness. At this level of conscientization, the learner can more deeply interpret problems, think critically, is self-confident in discussions, and exhibits receptiveness, responsibility, and scrutiny of thought.

Learning and understanding are enhanced through activities that encourage learners to critically reflect on socio-cultural and life situations. Student affairs professionals can encourage journal writing, seminars, focus groups, and other methods to foster this type of reflective and critical thinking. Economics, criminal justice, history, education, and business courses all provide opportunities to explore Freire's concepts. Conscientization may provide mechanisms that are especially useful in empowering those learners on campus who have been traditionally oppressed. In Chapter 6 we discuss this theory in more detail as we explore service learning.

Summary

Theories of learning provide us with cues for linking student affairs to learning both inside and outside the classroom. As advisors, leaders, and guides we set contexts within which the learning of the classroom can crystallize. "The process of learning is located at the interface of people's biography and the sociocultural milieu in which they live . . ." (Jarvis, 1992, p. 17). College students have traditionally "played" much of their educational biographies in the classroom. The milieu in which they live is a colorful combination of social, athletic, academic, and artistic events. Often, these 'events' provide meaning for their classroom learning.

The theories that we have chosen to describe here are but a sampling of the wealth of knowledge about learning. For a more detailed discussion of these and other theories of learning see (Stage, Muller, Kinzie and Simmons, 1998). In the next chapter we focus on specific differences in learning across cultural groups. As we turn to our own campuses, we suggest that attention be directed squarely on theories of learning. There we can continue to do what we do best, provide environments that maximize opportunities for learning.

References

American College Personnel Association (ACPA). (1994). *The student learning imperative: Implications for student affairs.* Washington, DC: Author.

Anderson, J. (1988). Cognitive styles and multicultural populations. *Journal of Teacher Education, 39*(1), 2–9.

Bandura, A. (1986). *Social foundations of thought and action: A social cognitive theory*. Englewood Cliffs, NJ: Prentice-Hall.

Bandura, A. (1993). Perceived self-efficacy in cognitive development and functioning. *Educational Psychologist, 28*, 117–148.

Bandura, A. (1994). Self-efficacy. In V. S. Ramachaudran (Ed.), *Encyclopedia of Human Behavior* (Vol. 4, pp. 71–81). New York: Academic Press.

Bandura, A. (1997). *Self-efficacy: The exercise of control*. New York: Freeman.

Belenky, M., Clinchy, B. Goldberger, N. and Tarule, J. (1986). *Women's ways of knowing*. New York: Basic Books.

Chickering, A. W. and Gamson, Z. F. (1987). Seven good practices in undergraduate education. *AAHE Bulletin, 39*(7), 3–7.

Driver, R., Asoko, H., Leach, J., Mortimer, E., and Scott, P. (1994). Constructing scientific knowledge in the classroom. *Educational Researcher, 23*(7), 5–12.

Friere, P. (1970). *Pedagogy of the oppressed*. New York: Herder and Herder.

Gardner, H. (1983). *Frames of Mind*. New York: Basic Books.

Gardner, H. and Hatch, T. (1989). Multiple intelligences go to school. *Educational Researcher, 18*(8), 4–9.

Gilligan, C. (1982). *In a different voice: Psychological theory and women's development*. Cambridge, MA: Harvard University Press.

Glover, J. A., Ronning, R. A. and Bruning, R. H. (1990). *Cognitive psychology for teachers*. New York: MacMillan Publishing Company.

Jarvis, P. (1992). *Paradoxes of learning: On becoming an individual in society*. San Francisco: Jossey-Bass.

Kitchener, K. and King, P. (1990). The reflective judgement model: Ten years of research. In M. Commons, C. Armon, L. Kohlberg, R. Richards, T. Grotzer, and J. Sinnott (Eds.), *Adult development: Models and methods in the study of adolescent and adult thought*. New York: Praeger.

Kohlberg, L. (1981). *The meaning and measurement of moral development*. Worcester, MA: Clark University Press.

Kolb, D. A. (1981). Learning styles and disciplinary differences. In A. W. Chickering and Associates (Eds.), *The modern American college* (232–255). San Francisco: Jossey-Bass.

Perry, W. (1981). Cognitive and ethical growth: The making of meaning. In A. Chickering and Associates (Eds.), *The modern American college* (76–116). San Francisco: Jossey-Bass.

Pressley, M. and Mcormick, C. B. (1995). *Advanced educational psychology for educators, researchers, and policymakers.* New York: HarperCollins.

Rothschadl, A. M. and Russell, R. V. (1992). Improving teaching effectiveness: Addressing modes of learning in the college classroom. *Schole: A Journal of Recreation Education and Leisure Studies, 7.*

Russell, R. V. and Rothschadl, A. M. (1991). Learning styles: Another view of the college classroom? *Schole: A Journal of Recreation Education and Leisure Studies, 6.*

Skinner, B. F. (1953). *Science and human behavior.* New York: Macmillan.

Skinner, B. F. (1968). *The technology of teaching.* New York: Appleton-Century-Crofts.

Stage, F. K. (1991). Common elements of theory: A framework for college student development. *Journal of College Student Development, 32,* 56–61.

Stage, F. K. (1996). Setting the context: Psychological theories of learning. *Journal of College Student Development, 27*(2), 227–235.

Stage, F. K. and Milne, N. V. (1996). 'Invisible scholars': College students with learning disabilities. *Journal of Higher Education.*

Stage, F. K., Muller, P., Kinzie, J. and Simmons, A. (1998). *Creating Learning Centered Classrooms: What Does Learning Theory Have to Say?* Washington, D.C.: ASHE/ERIC Reader Series.

Watson, L. (1996). A collaborative approach to student learning: A model for administrators in higher education. *Planning and Changing: An Educational Leadership and Policy Journal.*

3

Cultural Differences in Student Learning

Lemuel W. Watson
Melvin C. Terrell

This chapter provides a brief introduction to the differences that exist in learning among culturally diverse groups of students. We begin with a rationale detailing why understanding the differences between underrepresented minority students, culturally diverse students, and majority students is important. We provide some analysis of the preferred learning styles of various groups of students. In addition, incorporation of such information into the campus community is discussed.

As we begin to accept the fact that our American educational system is not perfect for all, we discover that aspects of the curriculum and some teaching methods could be changed to respond to the various needs of today's students. It is no secret that the long-standing tradition of American education has been to resist the input of subcultures and to strive for the production of the "model American" through a formal schooling process. For the most part, the direction charted by America's formal teaching methods and curriculum has been "standard American"—middle-class White, Anglo-Saxon, and Protestant (Fain, Shostak, and Dean, 1979).

For example, learning styles of students (briefly mentioned in

Chapter 2) have been studied at the early childhood stage. Students learn how to process information at an early age and that process is influenced by a number of factors including language and culture. In more detail, Heath (1983) described how specific languages in communities influence students' learning styles. For example, in community "A," students learned through story-telling as a main avenue to process information. Children were en-couraged to enhance their storytelling with exaggerations and elabo-rations to make their version exciting. Community "B" used visual materials, adult, and Biblical stories to teach. In this community, getting the facts correct was emphasized. Third, community "C" taught children to relate events in their lives to the many types of books they read.

As these groups of students entered the educational system, the first community's students had a difficult time in seeing the connec-tion between a story in a book and their own lives. In addition, the teacher could not understand why these students would add their own twists to the stories. When students from community "B" were asked to fantasize or predict what they thought would have happen from the text they read, they were resistant because they perceived this as not in keeping with the "facts" of the story; which is how they were taught. Finally, children from community "C," middle-class families, tended to be in the top reading groups and made the great-est progress in understanding the material because their style of learn-ing is preferred in most school systems (Heath, 1983; Wertsch and Kanner, 1994).

Heath concluded that environmental factors, communities, and families have a tremendous impact on learning styles. In fact, the communication between teacher and student becomes a significant influence in the student's educational gains. She suggested that many children "fail" not because they function poorly in some absolute sense, but because teachers' lack of awareness of different language variants hinders their ability to engage children in the classroom to enhance their development (Heath, 1993; Wertsch and Kanner, 1994). In fact, Heath's findings provide evidence of the ways that Bourdieu and Passeron's (1990) description of cultural capital (described in Chapter 1) supports middle- and upper-class students as they enter the educational system. Given the poor rate of retention for minority college students (Fleming, 1984; Padilla, Trevino, Gonzalez and Tre-vino, 1997) we might speculate that educators and professionals in higher education continue to experience similar situations regarding language and cultural and generational barriers (Anderson, 1988; Botstein, 1991; Cook and Helms, 1991; Jones, Terrell and Duggar, 1991).

A major and growing body of students that has historically been disadvantaged by American society and academia includes culturally diverse groups such as African-Americans, Hispanic-Americans, Asian-Americans, and Native Americans. Dunn, Beasley and Buchanan (1994) reported that changing demographics in American schools show that the current "minority" population will become a majority in 53 of our largest cities over the next five years. While there have been many efforts to provide equity in education for culturally diverse students, the preponderance of settings remain troublesome and unaccommodating at best (Allen and Boykin, 1992; Hale-Benson, 1986; Ladson-Billings, 1992; Lomotey, 1992; Rhodes, 1994; Smith, 1992; Terrell, 1992; Wilson and Carter, 1988).

Yet, as educators and professionals we continue to require our students to fit a system that needs to be updated and repaired. We now have students who enroll in our institutions with diverse styles of learning that are difficult to identify at a glance. Because institutions fail to incorporate the learning styles of many students including culturally diverse students, those students continue to be marginalized in the campus community (Atkinson, Morten, and Sue 1989; Cook and Helms, 1991). In fact, one recent study reveals that minority students may invest more effort than majority students in campus activities, both in class and out of class, and continue to reap fewer educational gains than their peers (Watson, 1994; Watson and Kuh, 1996). Such studies reveal the inequities that exist for ethnic minority students on predominantly white campuses (Fleming, 1984; Watson and Kuh, 1996). Therefore, as suggested in Chapter 1, a wholistic approach to intellectual development and learning styles begins with the assumption that cognitive processing must be considered in cultural, historical, and institutional contexts (Knefelkamp and Associates, 1978; Stage and Manning, 1992; Terrell, 1992; Vygotsky, 1981; Watson, 1996; Wertsch and Kanner, 1994).

Culturally Diverse Learning Styles

Learning styles of specific cultural groups are described in the literature in varying degrees and some data point out that there is great individual diversity within cultural groups as well (Anderson, 1988;

Stage and Manning, 1992). Some evidence exists that efforts to accommodate these differences in the academic world brings improved
learning achievement levels (Dunn, Beasley and Buchanan, 1994;
Griggs and Dunn, 1989; Herring, 1992; Hodson, 1993; Hilliard III,
1992; Rakow and Bermudez, 1993; Ross-Gordon, 1991; Smith, 1992;
Valencia, 1992). According to the framework in Chapter 1, learning
styles can be considered as input factors because such data provide
information for planning services, programs, and curricula to enhance
students' educational gains. By understanding learning styles, we are
able to connect with and motivate our students to become involved
and invested in their educational experiences.

While it is important to understand common patterns of learning, we focus more specifically on differences in cognitive functioning and how individuals within various cultures process, organize,
and retrieve information. The classifications listed below are not in
contradiction to theories presented by Stage and Muller in Chapter
2, but provide different ways of viewing students' learning styles.
Our primary focus is the Dunn and Griggs model of learning styles
that categorizes major cognitive process into psychological, sociological, emotional, physiological and environmental elements (Dunn and
Griggs, 1990). From the literature, we have categorized the characteristic of learning styles for specific cultural groups into three com-
monly used classifications: Field Dependent vs. Field Independent;
Physiological; and Environmental.

Field Dependent vs. Field Independent

Field Dependency includes psychological, sociological and emotional styles of learning and has been described as having relational,
affective, global, and impulsive characteristics. It is also characterized by a self and people orientation, group and cooperative learning
orientations and employs intuitive analysis and synthesis of information with less accuracy while personalizing information to understand
concepts. A field-dependent person is often emotional and expres-
sive in communications; in harmony with nature, community, and
family; sees time as flexible and subjective; seeks personal relevance
when processing information; and thinks wholistically. These characteristics have been attributed primarily to right brain hemispheric capability (Dunn and Griggs, 1990).

On the other hand, field independence has been described as
analytical, non-affective, sequential, linear, reflective (taking longer

to conclude but having more accuracy), stimulus-centered and parts-specific, characterized by long attention and concentration spans. It often involves abstract principles for stimuli, learning material that is inanimate and impersonal and the removal of self from situations. An individual that breaks the whole into parts to analyze shows field independence and generally the opposite is true of a field-dependent individual. These characteristics have been attributed primarily to left brain hemispheric capability (Dunn and Griggs, 1990).

The literature describes African-Americans and Hispanic-Americans primarily as field-dependent learners as opposed to Western European Americans who are described as predominantly field independent. Academic America primarily offers curricula and instructional methods that cater to the field-independent learner (Anderson, 1988; Dunn and Griggs, 1990).

African-Americans' style of learning has been reported as predominantly self- or person-centered (focused on personal or social cues in learning and problem solving), people-oriented, with a preference for social issues and a view to bringing all the parts to a whole for analysis. This approach is non-analytic and employs interpersonal communication such as "I" or "we" instead of third person. Intuitive analysis and synthesis factors play heavily in knowledge acquisition style (Bell, 1994, Griggs and Dunn, 1989, Garza, 1978).

Hispanic-Americans' learning style (while varying with sub-cultures) has been reported as affective, group oriented with a tendency to think deductively, placing emphasis on conformity and solidarity, and responsivity to family expectations rather than to self-directed goals. Interpersonal relations, human-relations, and being person centered are important. Open acceptance of affective temperament and a significant preference for role models from one's own culture characterizes Hispanics' learning styles (Rakow and Bermudez, 1993; Arciniega and Arrigo, 1981; Garza, 1978).

The Asian-American style of learning has been described as quite distinctive; and characteristics between and within subcultures can be very individualistic. Specifically, Cantonese-Chinese and South Asians were found to be field independent in Britain and the U.S., but with a trend toward field dependency in their own country (More, 1990). Japanese students show strong preferences for intuition and creativity or right hemisphere brain activity, and for planning and precision, which is left brain activity. Kuwaiti students showed strong left brain activity (Soliman and Torrance, 1986). Chinese students (in China) showed a strong preference for individual study as opposed to group study (Melton, 1990).

Native Americans' styles of learning have been described as different among the sub-cultures, but still with some commonalties. More (1990) found that Native American migratory hunters were field independent while agricultural groups were field dependent individuals. However, as a whole, the culture was more reflective in learning style. Other styles that have been attributed to the Native American culture indicate that they are cooperative with others, but competitive with their own personal performance while showing preference to learn from familiar materials. They value a harmonious relationship with nature, and leadership based on outstanding ability and respect (Smith, 1992, Herring, 1992).

Additionally, some theories that were developed specifically for general college student populations bear brief discussion here. Chapter 2 describes a model of cognitive processes based on Kolb's (1981) and Anderson's (1988) work. Kolb's typology consists of four types of learning styles: (a) convergers, (b) divergers, (c) assimilators, and (d) accommodators. Within this typology culturally diverse students are often classified as divergers seeking concrete experiences and practice, compared to majority students who are assimilators and favor abstract and reflective thinking. Chapter 2 gives an overview of how such orientations of learning styles can affect educational outcomes. Additionally, Anderson (1988) and Stage (1996) reiterate the fact that students' success is dependent, for the most part, on how well they understand the academic coursework. Because outcomes of academic coursework are closely tied to students' self-efficacy (Chapter 2), failure or success affects how they perceive their place within the university community, ultimately affecting educational gains as illustrated in the conceptual framework in Chapter 1.

Physiological Classification

Physiological elements of learning include perceptual (visual, auditory, kinesthetic, oral), intake (eating, drinking), time, and mobility. Cultural differences in learning styles for each group for this element are described below (Bell, 1994; More, 1990; Rakow and Bermudez, 1993).

African-Americans' learning styles can include use of culturally-altered English terms and interpretations, symbolic imagery such as use of words, metaphors and proverbs, gestures, rhythms, dance, music, and song to construct and express knowledge conveying multiple meanings. In addition, African-Americans prefer to learn in an environment that has diverse stimuli, response vibrancy, frequent breaks from tasks, and strong and colorful expression. Some students may respond poorly to timed, scheduled, preplanned activities that interfere with immediacy of response (Bell, 1994, Sandhu, 1994, Hodson, 1993, Hunt, 1993, Hale-Benson, 1986).

Hispanic-American learning styles show a preference for non-verbal communication. Additionally, not maintaining eye contact with superiors and other culturally specific gestures related to interaction can complicate communication on campus. The most significant culturally diverse element for this group is language. New subjects or technology being introduced to a cultural group that is already dealing with the second-language concept compounds the problem of learning. Rakow and Bermudez (1993) point out that a lack of one-to-one correspondence between English and Spanish words and differences between regional dialects further complicates learning for this group. An interesting sidenote indicates that it takes approximately seven years to master the necessary cognitive and academic language proficiency to successfully master instruction in a content area and that most students spend no more than two years in English as a second language (Arciniega and Arrigo, 1981; Rakow and Bermudez, 1993).

Often Asian-Americans have learning styles that prefer visual spatial images or graphic representations, verbal modes and spatial reasoning skill, and spatial memory (More, 1990; Soliman and Torrance, 1986). Language diversity issues for Asian-Americans are similar to those for Hispanics.

Native Americans' learning styles include oral language and imagery to express many thoughts in graphic similes and natural-world metaphors, non-verbal communication, and spatial, visual, and visual perceptual strengths (Herring, 1992; More, 1990). Language in the Native American culture has not been noted in the literature as an area of diversity in academic learning situations.

Environmental Elements

Environmental learning variables include sound, light, temperature and design. Griggs and Dunn (1989) found specific cultural preferences in the Learning Style Profile study including: African-Americans preferences are reported to be better able to learn under cooler temperature conditions, employing hands-on learning and through formal study arrangements. Hispanic-Americans preferences are for warmer temperatures, dim lights, and freedom to move about and take breaks. Asian-Americans showed a preference for study during late morning hours. Native Americans showed preference for informal learning situations, flexible curricular designs, sound to muffle outside distractions, and bright light conditions. Obviously, the ideal learning environment for a diverse group of students is impossible to create. But varying learning tasks and conditions might provide for a broader range of student learning in classes.

Implications

Probably the most important conclusion to be drawn from the three elements of learning is that cognitive processing is greatly influenced by the cultural history of a student (Anderson, 1988; Dunn and Griggs, 1990). It is also important to recognize that variation of these three elements within a cultural group may be as great as variation across groups. So we cannot make assumptions about learning and based on a students' culture or ethnicity. The point is that by being aware of such differences among students we can design courses that incorporate many kinds of learning (Stage, Muller, Kinzie, and Simmons, 1998). We should examine educational environments that employ the learning styles associated only with Western culture and encourage institutions to broaden their curricula and the expertise of their faculty to adapt and incorporate multiple approaches to learning so that all students may have an equitable chance to reap maximum educational outcomes. Motivation of any student to learn is related to the opportunity they have to learn in their own distinctive preferred manner. Motivation can be greatly enhanced among diverse groups of students as educators become aware of specific differences in how students learn and by adapting their instructional methods and employing culturally oriented materials (Stage, Muller, Kinzie, and Simmons, 1998).

Motivation to learn can be enhanced by successful activity—that is, achieving levels of knowledge that match intent or expectation. Smith's (1992) study of Navajo children, described children's eyes lighting up with excitement when they saw a program that had familiar pictures and references. Allen and Boykin (1992) conducted a series of studies that showed significantly enhanced performances by Black children when they were taught using culturally specific materials and methods. They projected that cultural discontinuity in the educational system could be a major contributor to the staggering academic failures that exist today for culturally diverse students, and suggested that prescriptive pedagogy could help alleviate this condition.

Lomotey (1992) reported on the successful operation of African centered educational institutions. Council of Independent Black Institutions (CIBI) students have been shown to attain a high level of self-esteem and to perform better academically as measured by standard achievement tests. Rakow and Bermudez (1993) conducted surveys of teachers to identify their handling of Hispanic-American students as a diverse culture. Not surprisingly, the teachers often made no distinction between cultures in their teaching style or curriculum.

Rakow and Bermudez reported that different cultures have diverse learning needs and that the treatment of the specific groups could be a part of the problem of low participation rates for some cultural groups in science and math. In support of this finding, Anderson (1988) reported culturally diverse students have more difficulty with mathematics and the hard sciences where theory precedes the practical application—an abstract versus a concrete learning style. In addition, Rhodes (1994) concluded in his article on Navajo families and Navajo culture that it does not make much sense to expect Navajo students to change their values and ways of thinking to fit a "foreign" schooling system. It makes more sense to restructure the system.

Enhancing Learning through Practical Models

The preponderance of literature reviewed indicated that offering culture-oriented education and teaching accommodation for the preferred learning styles of culturally diverse students would significantly enhance learning success. A program designed to accomplish a "culturally democratic" classroom and accomplish the objectives of culture orientation and accommodation was outlined by Sandhu (1994) as a three-step process that would be carried out by culturally responsive educators and professionals.

1. Awareness

Actively seek knowledge about other cultures and ethnic groups through all means available. Learn how to create equitable learning conditions for students who are from diverse ethnic backgrounds.

Examine your own beliefs, values, and behaviors as to how they might have positive or negative effects upon culturally different/ distinct students. For example, as student affairs professionals we may use the opportunity of orientation programs to assess student learning styles and report that information to the university community.

2. Acceptance

Accept the notion that cultural diversity is an asset, a strength that makes America great. Accept the notion that all students can learn. Believe that all students have potential to excel in the areas of their interest, respect divergent thinking and different viewpoints of students.

3. Action

Empower students through personal attention, encouragement and support. Practice behaviors that are free from prejudice, bias, and stereotypes and also encourage students to do so. Be genuine, considerate and empathic with students both in and outside the classroom. Be committed to promote cultural diversity and be open to new experiences and challenges. Often we make assumptions about how our programs, services, and curricula should be designed based on our own experiences. We work on the notion that we know what is best for the students. However, each new generation of students can teach us something about their uniqueness. Although we have the responsibility to assist in the learning and development of students, we have much to learn from our students.

We would also like to encourage student affairs professionals to see themselves as cultural brokers. According to Stage and Manning (1992) the cultural broker model is characterized by a situation where:

- All participants work to create environments that embrace and support the institution in its movement from monoculturalism to multiculturalism;
- Student affairs educators exhibit leadership roles in the movement from monoculturalism to multiculturalism; and
- The institution is challenged in its fundamental way of conducting day-to-day business on campus, in the community, and throughout the world.

More specifically, Stage and Manning offer four practical items for cultural brokers to utilize in order to create environments that are open and just for all students.

1. *Learning to Think Contextually* requires us to recognize when and where cultural expectations and assumptions create dissonance for individuals.

2. *Span Boundaries* challenges us to move within other cultures in order to understand how to design programs and services to enhance the learning, involvement, and educational gains of all students.

3. *Ensure Optimal Performance* calls for us to form collaborative efforts with students and possibly other institutional agents to optimize strengths within the campus community through adaptations versus assimilation.

4. *Take Action* requires us to do something with the knowledge we have on creating an inclusive campus. We should become leaders in informing institutional agents of the unique differences that exist regarding student learning style. (Stage and Manning, 1992)

Conclusion

Creating a learning environment where all students may reach their fullest potential is not an easy task. This chapter presents a few characteristics that may be generalized to the learning styles of specific minority groups in institutions of higher education. However, there is no substitute for knowing and understanding cultural differences and nuances of one's own student body. Although we have much information from students' admission applications (high school, SAT scores, personal interests, etc.), we continue to lack knowledge regarding how minority college students are motivated to learn and to become actively involved in the college environment (process).

The dropout rate of minority students clearly points to a mismatch between them and some institutions of higher education (Terrell, 1992). This is a national problem and more specifically an educational problem that needs to be addressed by all educators in the near future. Increasing the rate of participation and success of minority students should be one of the most important goals for American higher education.

Input and process factors are directly related to the viability of our country through educated and productive citizens (an output factor). For example, if access to educational opportunity for minorities does not improve, a disproportionate percentage of students will continue to be condemned to lives of deprivation. Such conditions run counter to our national ideals and threaten the foundation of our democratic system because a continuation of inequities serves as a catalyst to social tensions and unrest. They also undermine our position in the global arena as both a moral force and an economic power (Angel and Barrera, 1991).

Enhancing educational outcomes is a growing concern across many college and university campuses. The role of student affairs may be pivotal in the willingness to interpret culturally diverse learning styles in the context of institutional missions and to encourage the allocation of resources (human and capital) on campuses. How institutions respond in changing to meet the challenges of minority learning styles may be directly related to the preparation of student affairs teams in recognizing the legitimacy of language styles, cultural nuances, and preferred styles of learning of populations that are not ill-prepared, just different. We should inform the campus community that learning styles play an important role in the educational gains of students. If we do not take the initiative for enhancing learning environments for students, who will?

References

Allen, B. A., and Boykin, W. A. (1992). African-American Children and the Educational Process: Alleviating Cultural Discontinuity Through Prescriptive Pedagogy. *School Psychology Review*, Vol. 21, No. 4, pp. 586–596.

Anderson, J. (1988). Cognitive styles and multicultural populations. Journal of Teacher Education, 39, pp. 2–9.

Arciniega, M., and Arrigo, A. (1981). A Theoretical Analysis of Hills Cognitive Style Inventory: Implications for Assessing Mexican Americans Preferred Learning Style (Part I). *Journal of Instructional Psychology*, Vol. 8, No. 1, pp. 2–9.

Atkinson, D, Morten, G., and Sue, D. (1989). *Counseling American Minorities: A Cross-Cultural Perspective*. Dubuque: Brown.

Angel, D. and Barrera, A. (Eds.). (1991). *Rekindling Minority Enrollment.* San Francisco: Jossey-Bass.

Bell, Y. R. (1994). A Culturally Sensitive Analysis of Black Learning Style. *Journal of Black Psychology,* Vol. 20, No. 1, pp. 47–61.

Botstein, L. (1991). The undergraduate curriculum and the issue of race. In P. Altbach and K. Lomotey (Eds.), *The Racial Crisis in Higher Education.* Albany: SUNY Press.

Bourdieu, P., and Passeron, J. (1990). *Reproduction in education, society and culture.* Beverly Hills: Sage.

Cook, D. and Helms, J. The role of counselors in combating the 'new racism' at predominantly White universities. In E. Herr, and J. McFadden (Eds.), *Challenges of Cultural and Racial Diversity to Counseling.* Alexandra: AACD Media.

Dunn, R., Beasley, M., and Buchanan, K. (1994). What Do you Believe About How Culturally Diverse Students Learn? *Emergency Librarian,* Vol. 22, No. 1, pp. 8–14.

Dunn, R., and Griggs, S. (1990). Research on the Learning Styles Characteristics of Selected Racial and Ethnic Groups. *Reading, Writing, and Learning Disabilities,* Vol. 6, pp. 261–280.

Fain, S., Shotak, R., and Dean J. (1979). *Teaching In America.* Glenview: Scott, Foresman and Company.

Fleming, J. (1984). *Blacks in College: A Comparative Study of Students' Success in Black and White Institutions.* San Francisco: Jossey-Bass.

Garza, R. T. (1978). Affective and Associative Qualities in the Learning Styles of Chicanos and Anglos. *Psychology in the Schools,* Vol. 15, No. 1, pp. 111-115.

Griggs, S., and Dunn, R. (1989). The Learning Styles of Multicultural Groups and Counseling Implications. *Journal of Multicultural Counseling and Development,* Vol. 17, pp. 146–155.

Hale-Benson, J. E. (1986). *Black Children: Their Roots, Culture, and Learning Styles.* Chapter 2. Baltimore and London: The Johns Hopkins University Press

Heath, S. (1983). *Ways with Words: Language, Life and Work in Communities and Classrooms.* New York: Cambridge University Press.

Herring, R. D. (1992). Seeking a New Paradigm: Counseling Native Americans. *Journal of Multicultural Counseling and Development,* Vol. 20, pp. 35–43.

Hilliard III, A. G. (1992). Behavioral Style, Culture, and Teaching and Learning. *Journal of Negro Education*, Vol. 61, No. 3, pp. 370–377.

Hodson, D. (1993). In Search of a Rationale for Multicultural Science Education. *Science Education*, Vol. 77, No. 6, pp. 685–711.

Hunt, S. (1993). Cultural Perspectives and Thinking: The African American Thinker in the Classroom. Paper presented at the Annual Meeting of the Speech Communication Association (79th, Miami Beach, Fla., November 18–21, 1993). Speeches/Conference paper (150), Info. Analyses (070), Viewpoints (Opinion/Position Papers, essays, etc.) (120), ED 368 017.

Jones A., Terrell, M., and Duggar, M. (1991). The role of student affairs in fostering cultural diversity in higher education. *NASPA Journal*, 28, pp 121–127.

Knefelkamp L. and Associates (1978). *Applying new developmental findings*. San Francisco: Jossey-Bass.

Kolb, D. A. (1981). Learning styles and disciplinary differences. In A. W. Chickering and Associates (Eds.), *The modern American college* (pp. 232–255). San Francisco: Jossey-Bass

Ladson-Billings, G. (1992). Liberatory Consequences of Literacy: A Case of Culturally Relevant Instruction for African American Students. Journal of Negro Education, Vol. 61, No. 3, pp. 378-391.

Lomotey, K. (1992). Independent Black Institutions: African-Centered Education Models. *Journal of Negro Education*, Vol. 61, No. 4, pp. 455–462.

Melton, C. D. (1990). Bridging the Cultural Gap: A Study of Chinese Students' Learning Style Preferences. RELC Journal, Vol. 21, No. 1, pp. 29–54.

More, A. J. (1990). Learning Styles of Native Americans and Asians. 22p.; Paper presented at the Annual Meeting of the American Psychology Assn. (98th), Boston, Ma., August 13, 1990). Info. Analyses (070), Speeches/Conference Papers (150), Ed 330 535.

Padilla, R. V., Trevino, J., Gonzalez, K. and Trevino, J. (1997). Developing local models of minority student success in college. *Journal of College Student Development*, 38(2), 125–135.

Rakow, S. J., and Bermudez, A. B. (1993). Science is "Ciencia" :Meeting the Needs of Hispanic American Students. *Science Education*, Vol. 77, No. 6, pp. 669–683.

Rhodes, R. W. (1994). A Navajo Education System for Navajo Students. *Journal of Navajo Education*, Vol. XII, No. 1, pp. 40–46.

Ross-Gordon, J. M. (1991). Needed: A Multicultural Perspective for Adult Education Research. *Adult Education Quarterly*, Vol. 42, No. 1, pp. 1–16.

Sandhu, D. S. (1994). Cultural Diversity in Classrooms: What Teachers Need to Know. Information Analyses (070), ED 370 911.

Soliman, A. M., and Torrance, P. E. (1986). Styles of Learning and Thinking of College Students in the Japanese, United States and Kuwait Cultures. *The Creative Child and Adult Quarterly*, Vol. XI, No. 4, pp. 196–204.

Smith, K. (1992). Using Multimedia with Navajo Children: An Effort to Alleviate Problems of Cultural Learning Style, Background of Experience and Motivation. *Reading and Writing Quarterly: Overcoming Learning Difficulties*, Vol. 8, pp. 287–294.

Stage, F. (1996). Setting the context: psychological theories of learning. *Journal of College Student Development*, Vol 37, pp. 227–235.

Stage, F. and Manning, K. (1992). *Enhancing the Multicultural Campus Environment: A Cultural Brokering Approach*, No. 60. Jossey-Bass: San Francisco.

Stage, F. K., Muller, P., Kinzie, J. and Simmons, A. (1998). *Creating Learning Centered Classrooms: What Does Learning Theory Have to Say?* Washington, D.C.: ASHE/ERIC Reader Series.

Terrell, M. (1992). *Diversity, disunity and campus community*. National Association of Student Personnel Administrators, Inc.

Vygotsky, L. (1981). The development of higher form of attention in childhood. In J. V. Wertsch (Ed.), *The Concept of Activity in Soviet Psychology*. Armonk: Sharpe.

Watson, L. (1994). *An Analysis of Black and White Students' Perceptions, Involvement, and Educational Gains in Private Historically Black and White Liberal Arts Institutions*. Unpublished doctoral dissertation, Indiana University, Bloomington, IN.

Watson, L. (1996). A collaborative approach to student learning: A model for administrators in higher education. *Planning and Changing: An Educational Leadership and Policy Journal*

Watson, L. and Kuh, G. (1996). The influence of dominant race environments on student involvement, perceptions, and educational gains: A look at Historically Black and Predominantly White liberal arts institutions. *Journal of College Student Development*, 37, pp. 415–424.

Wertsch, J. and Kanner, B. (1994). A sociocultural approach to intellectual development. In R. Sternberg and C. Berg (Eds.), *Intellectual Development*. New York: Cambridge University Press.

Wilson, R. and Carter, D. (1988). *Minorities in Higher Education: Seventh Annual Status Report*. Washington, DC: ACE.

4

Learning and Development from Theory to Practice

Michael J. Cuyjet
Leanne Lewis Newman

Professional educators concerned with the process of enhancing student learning will come, sooner or later, to the understanding that this development is wholistic, not solely focused on either the intellectual properties of learning or on the social context of personal behavior, but on the comprehensive growth of the whole person. According to Terenzini, Pascarella and Blimling (1996), those members of the academy who see students' academic and cognitive growth as the province of faculty and expect student affairs administrators to focus solely on enhancing students' affective growth subscribe to "functional and organizational dualism" (p. 149). This perception is in conflict with what we are beginning to understand about how students learn and develop wholistically. Many college and university student affairs practitioners are already aware of their significant role in providing an environment that can facilitate the opportunities for this "whole person" development. Such professionals are poised among the vanguard of educators engaged in the re-evaluation of the higher education learning process and that is necessary to prepare us for the challenges of the twenty-first century.

As Watson and Stage argue in Chapter 1, a re-examination of educational gains in light of the benefits to society and the resulting intergenerational effects is a critical component of the assessment of post-secondary education. Student affairs professionals who have honed their abilities to understand theories of learning, observe student experiences that manifest these theories, and make the critical link between theory and experiences will lead efforts to redefine student learning for tomorrow's students. The student affairs professional who understands theories of learning and development well enough to comprehend their practical applications in everyday campus situations can move beyond reacting to students' experiences. Such a person can intentionally create conditions that enhance student learning and personal development in a variety of settings throughout the campus environment.

In this spirit, this chapter will use a number of the theories and models described in the first two chapters of this book to examine ways in which these theoretical constructs can be applied to the daily activities of student affairs professionals in their efforts to enhance the learning and development of students. A number of hypothetical situations will be presented to exemplify these ideas. Then, four specific outcomes of theory-to-practice efforts—facilitating learning among the new students of the 90s, developing a sense of community living, use of values in learning and development, and instilling a service mindset among the institutional community—will be described and explained.

Practical Use of Theory

The Student Learning Imperative (SLI) (ACPA, 1994) that was introduced in Chapter 1 as a significant attempt to refocus student affairs personnel on their role in student learning draws particular emphasis on the marriage of theory and practice. The SLI is based on a number of assumptions about higher education, student affairs, and student development, including: students develop complex cognitive skills, practical competence skills, and an integrated sense of identity; learning, personal development, and student development are inextricably intertwined; and learning and development occur through transactions between students and their environments.

The person-environment and involvement theories of Chapter 1 and the developmental and learning theories of Chapter 2 contribute significantly to an understanding of these perceptions. For example, learning theories explore processes whereby ideas and concepts are interpreted; psychosocial theories describe skill development; person-environment interaction theories, campus ecology theory, and student involvement theory teach about student transactions with the environment and the benefits that derive from them. Student affairs professionals are not necessarily expected to retain the structures and components of all these theories in their minds at all times.

However, an understanding of the basic foci of a representative sample of these theories can be useful while addressing the student needs that student affairs professionals are likely to encounter daily. After all, what we identify as behavioral theories began as the recordings of repeated, careful observations of groups of people. By identifying patterns of behavior, it became possible to speculate, with some accuracy, how other, similar individuals may act. Like a physician who can identify symptoms and thus anticipate an individual's health status and prescribe remedial actions to move the individual toward better health, student affairs professionals can use theory to portend developmental status and prescribe appropriate actions to assist the individual in advancing that development. And, as Stage and Muller in Chapter 2 and McEwen (1996) point out, an additional benefit to the contemporary use of theory on the campus is that it provides ground for communication for student affairs professionals and faculty.

Use of Developmental Theories

Chapter 2 briefly summarizes a number of cognitive development theories with which student affairs professionals have become familiar and that have some practical application in the campus environment. The following are several brief scenarios that provide examples of situations in which a utilitarian, working knowledge of these theories—Perry's (1970) perspective on intellectual and cognitive development, Kohlberg's (1975) and Gilligan's (1993) views on moral reasoning, and King and Kitchener's (1994) theory of reflective judgment—could benefit the student affairs professional and the students he/she serves.

A residence hall director encounters a conflict between two roommates in which one of the parties adamantly refuses to see the other's perception of a particular incident. One roommate has taken a CD belonging to the other without asking permission. The second views this as stealing, plain and simple, and refuses to listen to protestations that the CD was merely borrowed. By recognizing the second student's perspective as dualistic thinking (Perry, 1970) about the absolute wrongness of the "theft," the resident director can attempt to expose this individual to the possibility that multiple viewpoints exist and one or more of these other viewpoints might have some validity.

An irate commuter student storms into the office of the parking division of the campus police on the first day of classes, demanding to know why the dozens of illegally parked cars in his lot are not being ticketed. If he can inconvenience himself enough to memorize and observe all the parking regulations, anyone who chooses not to do so should be punished appropriately. The officer's ability to identify a conventional "law and order" orientation according to Kohlberg's (1975) theory of moral reasoning might help him attempt to calm the individual and persuade him (as Kohlberg's postconventional reasoning would allow) that officers need to be permitted to alter regulations to accommodate social utility.

The faculty advisor to the All Greek Council is approached by the current president, a woman, who is upset by criticism from the immediate past president, a man, who claims that she is not tough enough and displays weak leadership. He berated her because he feels she does not demand strict adherence to prescribed duties and responsibilities among the other organization officers and spends to much time "coddling" them. The advisor, familiar with Gilligan's (1993) theory of caring tendencies within feminine perspectives, explains to the young woman that leadership built on relationship development is just as valid and effective in many situations as a judgmental, authoritarian style of leadership with which her predecessor may be comfortable.

A student seeking advice at the Career Center indicates that she wants to be a physician because that is what her parents want but is frustrated because she is doing poorly in her science courses. When confronted with the reality of her science grades, she reiterates the certainty that she will become a doctor and, regarding her lack of ability in science classes, simply "dismisses" her need for a science background. The career counselor who recognizes this as stage three reasoning in King and Kitchener's (1994) model of reflective judgment can work with this student to help her understand that at stage three one tends, erroneously, to dismiss as irrelevant that which is not in agreement with one's own knowledge or is not obtained from authorities (her parents). The professional can also attempt to move her to the quasi-reflective thinking of stage four at which point she could acknowledge that her lack of academic success in certain classes presents an "ill-structured" problem for her career decision-making and that there is an element of uncertainty in choosing her vocational path.

Use of Learning Theories

As indicated in Chapter 2, a cursory comprehension of a number of theories related to learning are important to the student affairs professional who wishes to facilitate the development of the students with whom he/she interacts. Among the learning theories described are Skinner's cognitive approach to learning, Bandura's self-efficacy beliefs, Gardner's multiple intelligences, and Kolb's typology of learning styles. There are a number of ways in which the student affairs professional might apply these learning theories to students in co-curricular settings.

For example, an understanding of Skinner's (1953) principles of cognitive learning allow the student affairs professional to contribute to student learning on two levels. First, providing cognitive information in the co-curricular settings contributes to the students' overall store of knowledge by giving the student more data with which to function. Second, activities in which students engage in the co-curriculum can be structured to provide opportunities for students to interpret from and experiment with the cognitive knowledge they have accumulated in both their classroom and out-of-class experiences, providing a working laboratory for learning and employing what has been learned.

Bandura's (1993) theory of self-efficacy provides a strong theoretical foundation for student affairs professionals' efforts in providing students with myriad opportunities to experiment with their leadership and decision making abilities. Learning how to assess one's skills, how to exercise control over one's own level of functioning, and to exert influence over those external events that affect one's own life are parts of this critical ability.

More and more critical theorists and other academicians in sociology and similar disciplines tend to focus mainly on displays of logical-mathematical and linguistic intelligence, student affairs professionals are often in a position to provide students with opportunities to demonstrate and develop manifestations of the other of Gardner's (1993) seven intelligences—musical intelligence, spatial intelligence, bodily-kinesthetic intelligence, interpersonal intelligence, and intrapersonal intelligence. As Stage and Muller indicated in Chapter 2, these five other intelligences are traditionally undervalued in educational systems. Those who would assist students to develop their abilities have the opportunity to employ skills correlated with these other forms of thinking. Helping students to first identify these talents and then to perceive them as legitimate forms of intelligence may, in itself, be a tremendous enhancement of students' ability to learn.

Finally, a working knowledge of Kolb's (1981) typology of learning styles can serve the student affairs professional well in assisting students to find co-curricular experiences that are most suited to their particular learning styles, be they convergers, divergers, assimilators or accommodators (See Chapter 2). Additionally, the compatibility (or possibly, more importantly, the incompatibility) among learning styles of student leaders with each other and their compatibility with advisors and sponsors can be acknowledged to the benefit of the students under the watchful eye of a well-informed student affairs professional.

None of these examples of either developmental or learning theories are intended to offer evidence that students ought to be categorized, labeled and mentally filed away as specimen examples of various theory stages. The emphasis must be on simple identification for the purpose of fostering understanding and formulating a plan to provide developmental assistance. Rather than seeing theoretical knowledge as a metaphorical file cabinet in which one labels and files clients, one's working cognizance of theory could be seen as a toolbox from which the practitioner can select the proper instrument to address each particular problem or situation that calls for some assistance from the body of knowledge. Just as a mechanic would not use a hammer to fix every malfunction in a machine, a functional understanding of a variety of theories will allow the student affairs professional to be ready to address a wide range of developmental issues.

Support and Challenge

Professional practice involves providing supports, challenges, and resources to students. One of the easiest ways to understand this is in the context of Sanford's (1966) concept of challenge and support. Sanford suggests that both challenge and support must be present for development to occur. A lack of challenge allows the student to feel safe and not move toward growth. Conversely, too much challenge without adequate support causes retreat and maladaptive responses. Thus, the student's ability to accept challenge is contingent on the amount of support available. By using theoretical constructs and stage models as a guide, student affairs professionals can provide situations that challenge students intellectually, morally, ethically, and in their interpersonal interactions. However, it is critical that student affairs professionals also supply appropriate support in the form of helping individuals and supplying programs and tangible resources so students will make use of these opportunities to learn about themselves and their environment and to grow with that knowledge. We close with some specific examples of pertinent supports, challenges, and resources will be addressed with four theory-to-practice outcomes.

Four Specific Outcomes for Today's Practitioners

While numerous opportunities exist for student affairs practitioners to use theory in their day-to-day professional lives, four broad issues have emerged as being among the most significant topics of the current decade relating to the development of students on campuses across the country. The remainder of this chapter will explore the use of theory to devise relevant, practical ways to address four concerns and issues of student affairs professionals: identifying and meeting the needs of today's "new" students, developing community, instilling values, and fostering a service mindset.

Facilitating "New" Students

Twenty years after Barna, Haws, and Knefelkamp (1978) discussed issues facing the "new student," a newer and more different student is emerging for the late 1990s and the beginning of the twenty-first century. "American higher education has a history of being both responsive to the needs of the society it serves and reflective of the changing nature of that society" (p. 107). Higher education has shaped and been shaped by the needs of society.

A look at today's society helps define the "new" student of the next millennium. Just as the theories discussed provide a framework for practice, so, too, must the student affairs professional link that knowledge to the student of today. Stage (1991) bemoans the fact that despite the known profiles of today's student, a lapse exists from the theoretical knowledge to the practical use. Consequently higher education has a relatively impressive void to fill as the new students pass through its doors.

The "new" students for the coming years into the next millennium can be defined as part of a wider and more diverse population. These students will not only represent a tremendous variety of ethnic cultures, social backgrounds, and lifestyles; but they also will vary greatly in age and developmental needs. As such, multiculturalism must continue to be a goal of higher education. A useful definition of multiculturalism as it applies to these new students, emphasizes "communication, knowledge of different cultures, and appreciation and celebration of differences. An organization that is multicultural, understood as a dynamic interplay between and among cultures, can be productive, effective and inclusive" (Manning and Coleman-Boatwright, 1991, p. 367). The movement toward multiculturalism has inherent human rights and moral purposes, and it also serves a practical purpose of making the institution more effective because all members are affirmed and fulfilled (Manning and Coleman-Boatwright, 1991).

In addition to identifying diverse populations, practitioners must apply their theoretical knowledge toward the goal of maintaining sensitivity to those various campus groups. Different populations potentially learn and develop with different methods and may not fall into the mainstream of the college campus. Maintaining a healthy balance of multiculturalism within the framework of the campus as a whole community will be a challenge for student affairs professionals.

For example, more influence on the nature of programs for international students must be emphasized. Research on internationals shows that they merit services and support (Parr, Bradley, and Bingi, 1992). In the 1983–84 academic year, 340,000 international students attended American institutions of higher education. Estimates for the 1990s place the enrollments at more than one million. Moreover, more than one-fourth of the graduate students enrolled in the late 1990s can be expected to be international students. Special concerns of international students include meeting the needs of both their nuclear families and extended families, learning how to adapt to and respond to aspects of the American culture (such as assertiveness and competitiveness) adapting to American norms without compromising their own cultural norms, finding an adviser who will devote time to them, understanding class lectures, and confronting racial discrimination if they are perceived as non-white by American racial standards (Parr, Bradley, and Bingi, 1992). Parr et. al. also indicate that internationals seem willing to utilize the services of student affairs offices for assistance in addressing these concerns. With basic training and theoretical knowledge about internationals, student affairs professional and paraprofessional staff could become quite productive in serving as peer counselors and leaders for support groups. American universities continue to serve as the post-graduate education system for the world. As this trend continues, student affairs professionals will have to cater to the needs of the older international graduate students as well as undergraduate international students.

Needs of the older "new" or returning student will continue to be a growing area in which student affairs professionals may utilize their theoretical knowledge of learning and development (Terrell, 1990). Continuing education programs need to be available to older students who wish to return either to earn a degree or to become more professionally proficient. Recent growth in these programs must be accelerated and supported. Emphasis on assisting the older adult to return will become part of the mission of most institutions. Providing for the needs and interests of the older non-traditional student, degree-seeking or not, has and will consistently fall to student affairs practitioners.

The needs of older non-traditional students will change the focus of student activities as well. New older students require specific activities directed at their special interests and, while just as academically motivated, are not as motivated to take part in co-curricular or social activities as their younger counterparts (Pace, 1990). As this student population continues to grow, new challenges face student affairs professionals to include them in the overall program of the institution.

Though this is a small sample of the plethora of new students entering the college campus, it demonstrates the need to provide adequate supports and challenges for them to learn and develop as they matriculate and persist through the college environment. Grounded in theory, student affairs practitioners not only can provide the support to meet the challenges that these students face, but also can be active in the policy-making realm of their campuses to help facilitate their growth. With a broad theoretical base, sound logical arguments can be made that will ultimately enhance the collegiate experience of these students.

Developing Community

A second intended outcome of knowledge of theory is the ability to assist students to learn and develop within a community context. Certainly the collegiate experience extends beyond the classroom and into the co-curricular arena of students' lives. The college campus is a community where individuals go to class, talk with colleagues, challenge each other, and re-think previously entrenched positions, as well as eat, play, and if residential, sleep. Students must learn to live within this community. Through contact with others students learn and develop. They learn to live within a larger social context beyond their immediate circle of friends and acquaintances. They are part of a bigger picture. As student development professionals, we must be prepared to assist students to see themselves within that larger context.

Schroeder and Mable (1994) aptly focused on the educational potential of residence halls. In an environment of learning and development, residence hall living must continue to cater to new programs both formal and informal for the student. Residence hall living fosters sustained contact between students who differ from each other (Chickering and Reisser, 1993). In learning to understand diverse personalities and differences in people, students are able to develop integrity. Halls must emphasize co-curricular activities regarding women, minorities, and internationals as well as mainstream students.

In an age when campuses are beginning to cater to the needs of the commuter student, new opportunities and challenges await student affairs professionals. To pull nonresidential students into the college community it is especially important that practitioners be well-grounded in theory to facilitate the learning and development of this "Parking Lot to Class to Parking Lot" population. This growing campus population of non-residents not only has unique issues for learning and development, but can also provide a rich addition to the campus community milieu.

Theoretical knowledge can foster opportunities for students to participate broadly in the campus community outside their "micro-world." Accordingly, the campus community must offer myriad choices for attracting commuters to cocurricular involvement on the campus and for giving commuter students a sense of community within the college milieu. Examples include: music, dance, and the-atre performances that appeal to the tastes of non-traditional students; academic departmental and professional organizations specifically focused on assisting non-traditional student in preparing for new careers; and social organizations and clubs that cater to commuter students' interests and schedules. Additionally, service and service-learning opportunities should provide linkages between the campus and the neighboring communities in order to help commuting students bridge the college and non-college components of their lives. All of these opportunities must also include activities for students with families, so that they, too, may feel included as part of the campus community.

Further, the campus can extend itself into the broader communi-ty by extending invitations to non-faculty/non-student community members to take part in campus events. By expanding their activities beyond the campus' physical boundaries, students are able to partic-ipate in a truly interactive community and welcome others into it. Additionally, commuter students are able to include family and friends in their college lives.

Residential students also have the opportunity to learn and de-velop as they participate in the community beyond the campus. Na-tionwide, campuses are focusing on service-learning. While some have incorporated a service-learning component into the academic curric-ulum, many campuses also have community service as part of stu-dent organizational life. As students see the world beyond the campus and into the community, they are exposed to a variety of experiences they seldom have under other circumstances.

Developing Values

The Student Learning Imperative (ACPA, 1994) notes several assumptions about higher education. An underlying theme is that through the learning and development process, students will also adopt a value system based on their higher educational experience. Nota-bly, a college-educated person will have "a coherent integrated sense of identity, self-esteem, confidence, integrity, aesthetic sensibilities, and civic responsibilities" (ACPA, 1994). Adopting a value system goes beyond having a rigid belief system, but is movement "toward responsibility for self and others and the consistent ability to thoughtfully apply ethical principles" (Chickering and Reisser, 1993, p. 236), in other words, movement toward integrity.

The underlying theme of values in the SLI also places a burden upon the institution to provide ways to cultivate values. Mission statements should be the standard through which values are taught. What institutions value shapes what students value. The SLI compels us to ensure that student affairs professionals be "experts on students, their environments, and teaching and learning processes" (ACPA, 1994, p. 3). Theory-to-practice can be a vital source by which values can be taught and developed.

For example, character formation begins when values are modeled for students. This begins with a commitment to professionalism. By showing students what is valued in the work environment of the campus, valuing other professionals, staff, and students, and working toward building consensus and community, students learn values. Modeling values can also extend to pragmatic issues regarding multiple points of view.

An understanding of Perry's (1970) model of cognitive development can assist student affairs professionals as they work with students who may be dualists, seeing only right and wrong. In issues where multiple perspectives are presented with no clear-cut answer, student affairs professionals can assist students in understanding that value judgments must be made, not only to discern what is right for them, but also to understand that more that one perspective can be right. Modeling higher level values can be a powerful educational tool for instilling these values.

Additionally, institutions make value statements repeatedly in the policies and programming they choose to support. Though more intuitive, these messages can also make a tremendous impact as to what administrators believe to be important and what they want students to think is important. For example, policies that reflect basic ethical principles, such as respecting autonomy, benefitting others, doing no harm, being just, and being faithful (Kitchener, 1985), instill a strong sense of individual ethical behavior in the campus community. Additionally, programs that promote societal unity over individual rights make an important values statement about the importance of the total community's welfare. As student affairs professionals, we should examine our current policies and programs to determine what type of values statements we are sending to our students, particularly as related to diversity, inclusiveness, and acceptance of ethical responsibility.

Instilling a Service Mindset

As discussed, one of the most notable changes in the way institutions instill values is the shift of emphasis to "service." In a speech to the Association of American Colleges' meeting, the late Ernest L. Boyer, past president of the Carnegie Foundation for the Advancement of Teaching, described the growing sentiment that higher education is a "private benefit, not a public good" (1994, p. A48). In contrast to that feeling he enumerated several examples in which higher education goes beyond simply teaching and becomes involved in the everyday lives of people in the community. "Service . . . means far more than simply doing good, although that's [*sic*] important. Rather, it means that professors apply knowledge to real-life problems, use that experience to revise their theories, and become, in the words of professor Donald Schon at the Massachusetts Institute of Technology, 'reflective practitioners'" (Boyer, 1994, p. A48).

Boyer's plea for colleges of higher education to take "special pride in its capacity to connect thought to action, theory to practice," (p. A48) is compelling on many different levels. "Service" can become a mere catch-word if overused and underutilized. The "new" students, as they matriculate in the 1990s, will be affected by colleges incorporating "service" into their ways of thinking.

Institutions can view service along two avenues. First, colleges and universities should incorporate a service-mindedness toward students that will affect admissions, faculty, and curriculum. Secondly, institutions should emphasize service to the larger, outside world. (See Chapter 6 for a discussion of service learning in the context of theory.) While research, teaching and service have always characterized higher education, arguably research and teaching have received the most attention. In the 1990s, service should come to the forefront, and institutions must now develop, press for and stress service. What is service will be redefined, and the need for service will unleash upon the institution the need to change in those terms.

The opportunities and expectations for "service" leave a plethora of ways in which higher education can and will adapt. For example, at the University of Minnesota, "service" includes developing a new plan to meet the needs of the ever-changing student (Cage, 1994). The proposed plan would:

a. Make it easier for students to transfer into the institution;

b. Design financial-aid and tuition policies that ensure the recruitment, retention, and graduation of students;

c. Develop ways for students to build relationships with faculty and staff members; and

d. Increase on-campus housing as well as student activities and programs.

At Albertus Magnus College, "service" is a 3-year plan to assist students in getting a degree more quickly, thereby cutting educational costs as much as $11,500. Oberlin, Stanford, Middlebury College, Upper Iowa University and Valparaiso University are also in the process of meeting students' needs by offering special three-year degrees (Shea, 1994). Such decisions help raise or keep student enrollment, as well as help the student. Colleges and universities will pinpoint the changing trends of the new students and maintain an openness in exploring new avenues to assist students.

On the other hand, colleges will be in the business of educating students about service or how to serve, rather than be served. The university has an institutional obligation to bring the idea of service full circle. Service to the campus, to the immediate community, and to society are all elements to which students should be exposed by the campus that is serving them. Boyer says that undergraduates at colleges "would participate in field projects, relating ideas to real life. Classroom and laboratories would be extended to include health clinics, youth centers, schools, and government offices" (1994, p. A48). This model will in turn give dignity and status to the scholarship of service—of integrating and applying knowledge through service.

As institutions mature into this way of thinking, a new kind of student emerges. These new students not only see college as it was seen in the late 1970s, as a way to a better life (Barna, Haws, and Knefelkamp, 1978), but as a way of empowering themselves for what lies ahead in the world.

Most important, colleges and universities must encourage and train students to be stewards of the world in which they live. Some institutions have begun in recent years special volunteer and service agencies through which students can be exposed to the need for giving of oneself for the sake and betterment of the outside community. Baylor University in Waco, Texas, began a service program in the spring of 1985 called "Steppin' Out" in which members of all organizations including Greeks, professional, and honorary organizations were encouraged to take one day and spend it doing service projects in the community. The program has since grown into several special days throughout the year with a committee of students planning them. In addition, the university employs a full-time volunteer services director.

At Palm Beach Atlantic College, in West Palm Beach, Florida, one of the two founding principles of the college, that began in 1968, is called Workship. As the name implies, students must spend a portion of their college experience working in the surrounding community as a volunteer. Although no grade is assigned, a certain number of hours each year for four years is required for graduation. The value of the experience students receive as a result of such "mandatory volunteerism" can be noted in the number of students who ultimately choose careers based on their Workship placement, as well as being exposed to people and places with whom they would not come in contact under other conditions.

Conclusion

Clearly then, intended outcomes of using theory to practice models are wide and encompassing as they assist students to learn and develop. A broad range of theories and theoretical models— psychosocial, cognitive, ethical and moral, learning, challenge and support—are applicable to the college student population. Such theories and models can be useful in the design and delivery of programs that serve students' needs.

Theory can serve as the foundation for activities in two general areas—training of professional student affairs staff and faculty and cocurricular programming for students. The planning and especially the assessment (both pre- and post-event) of training programs for staff and faculty draw on theoretical models. Theoretical knowledge can also help facilitate the needs of the "new" student of the late 1990s and the new millennium, particularly non-traditional age students, ethnic minority students, and international students. In the remaining chapters, specific applications of the theories presented thus far are presented as a way of guiding campus applications.

Community living as part of the collegiate experiences provides out-of-classroom benefits. Using theory to assist students in developing a sense of community and a personal value system that corresponds with the value system of the institution is fundamental to development. Inherent in the practical manifestation of these learning and development theories is the creation of a service-learning mindset and a corresponding call to service, both modeled by student affairs professionals as well as instilled in students. Theories used in practice will be a key necessary ingredient for successful completion of both the institution's and the students' roles in the collegiate developmental process.

References

American College Personnel Association (ACPA). (1994). *The student learning imperative: Implications for student affairs.* Washington, D.C.: Author.

Bandura, A. (1993). Perceiving self-efficacy in cognitive development and functioning. *Educational Psychologist, 28,* 117–148.

Barna, A., Haws, J. R., and Knefelkamp, L. (1978). New students: Challenge to student affairs. In L. Knefelkamp, C. Widick, and C.A. Parker (Eds.) *New directions for student services* (No. 4): Applying new developmental findings (pp. 107–115). San Francisco: Jossey-Bass.

Boyer, E. L. (1994, March 9). Creating the new American college. *The Chronicle of Higher Education,* p. A48.

Cage, M. C. (1994, March 23). A struggle for reform. *The Chronicle of Higher Education,* pp. A41, A43.

Chickering, A. W., and Reisser, L. (1993). *Education and identity* (2nd Ed.). San Francisco: Jossey-Bass.

Gardner, H. (1993). *Multiple intelligences: The theory in practice.* New York: Basic books.

Gilligan, C. (1993). *In a different voice: Psychological theory and women's development.* Cambridge, MA: Harvard University Press.

King, P. M. and Kitchener, K. S. (1994). *Developing reflective judgment.* San Francisco: Jossey-Bass.

Kitchener, K. S. (1985). Ethical principles and ethical decisions in student affairs. In H. J. Canon and R. D. Brown (Eds.), *Applied ethics in student services* (New Directions for Student Services No. 30, pp. 17-30). San Francisco: Jossey-Bass. model. Unpublished manuscript. College Park, MD.

Kohlberg, L. (1975). The cognitive-developmental approach to moral education. *Phi Delta Kappan*, 56(1), 670–677.

Kolb, D. A. (1981). Learning styles and disciplinary differences. In A. W. Chickering and Associates (Eds.), *The modern American college* (pp. 232–255). San Francisco: Jossey-Bass.

Manning, K. and Coleman-Boatwright, P. (1991). Student affairs initiatives toward a multicultural university. *Journal of College Student Development*, 32, 367–374.

McEwen, M. K. (1996). The nature and uses of theory. In S. R. Komives and D. B. Woodard, Jr. (Eds.) *Student services: A handbook for the profession* (3rd ed., pp. 147–163). San Francisco: Jossey-Bass.

Pace, C. R. (1990). *The undergraduates: A report of their activities and progress in college in the 1980s.* Los Angeles: University of California, Center for the Study of Evaluation.

Parr, G., Bradley, L., and Bingi, R. (1992). Concerns and feelings of international students. *Journal of College Student Development*, 33, 20–25.

Perry, W. G., Jr. (1970). *Forms of intellectual and ethical development in the college years.* New York: Holt, Rinehart and Winston.

Sanford, N. (1966). *Self and society.* New York: Atherton.

Schroeder, C. C., and Mable, P. (Eds.). (1994). *Realizing the educational potential of residence halls.* San Francisco: Jossey-Bass.

Shea, C. (1994, March 30). Squeezing the calendar. *The Chronicle of Higher Education*, A35–A36.

Skinner, B. F. (1953). Science and human behavior. New York: Macmillan.

Stage, F. K. (1991). Common elements of theory: A framework for college student development. *Journal of College Student Development*, 32, 56–61.

Terenzini, P. T., Pascarella, E. T., and Blimling, G. S. (1996). Students' out-of-class experiences and their influence on learning and cognitive development: A literature review. *Journal of College Student Development*, 37, 149–162.

Terrell, P. S. (1990). Adapting institutions of higher education to serve adult students' needs. *NASPA Journal*, 32(2), 90–97.

5

Student Affairs and Learning in the Community College

Magdalena H. de la Teja
Diane F. Kramer

Awareness of purpose and mission is essential to fully understand student affairs and learning in the community college. In this chapter, we begin by proposing that community colleges reexamine their mission in order for student learning to become the primary focus.

Next we explore the characteristics of community college students and how these influence their involvement in learning activities, as well as institutional characteristics that promote or inhibit student motivation for involvement and learning. We examine the roles of student affairs professionals and describe partnerships with students, faculty, and academic administrators in *developing contexts* for student learning and personal development.

Finally, recommendations and conclusions about student affairs and learning in community colleges are summarized.

The Community College Mission and Learning

Since their inception in the early 1900s, community colleges have provided educational services to communities across the nation. Their mission to serve the educational, economic, and lifelong learning needs of the communities in which they are located has had a profound influence on the character of community colleges and has established for them a unique niche among institutions of higher education (Baker, Roueche, and Gillett-Karam, 1990; Cohen and Brawer, 1989). This mission distinguishes community colleges from four-year institutions, thereby providing diverse people with greater access to higher education.

More than fifty percent of all full-time, first-time students now begin their education at community colleges (Pierce, 1996; Seidman, 1995). Such access to higher education must continue to be a significant part of the community college purpose and is embodied in the "open door" admissions policy and the offering of comprehensive programs, including transfer curricula, occupational and technical programs, developmental and remedial education, and continuing education courses. The underlying assumption of the "open door" is that every person should have an opportunity to pursue a college education and that with individual quality of effort and adequate support services, each person can succeed.

Through their open door, community colleges attract students who for a variety of reasons may not successfully navigate the competitive admissions processes, or traditional settings of other institutions. As a result, the characteristics of community college students differ from traditional university students. As Watson and Stage discuss in Chapter 1, it is important to consider multiple factors in students' lives and the ways students' pre-college backgrounds influence their learning, involvement, and educational gains. Additionally, a variety of theories as noted by Stage and Muller in Chapter 2, such as self-efficacy (Bandura, 1986), social-constructivism (Driver, Asoko, Leach, Mortimer and Scott, 1994) and conscientization (Freire, 1970/1993) can inform the strategies of student affairs professionals, faculty, and academic administrators in facilitating the learning and personal development of their diverse student populations.

Community colleges are increasingly chosen to provide the training, re-training, and the technological skills required in local work forces—representatives from these groups often serve on advisory boards for the college's vocational programs. Because of this distinct role, community colleges are challenged to respond quickly to the changing needs of the business community, public schools, other colleges and agencies, and civic organizations. Such a relationship between town and gown enhances the learning environment for students on the college campus and extends their learning lab to the wider community. But to truly benefit from the town and gown relationship, community college educators also devote energy toward strengthening and expanding partnerships with these entities.

Some suggest that community colleges do not meet the learning needs of the under-prepared student sufficiently and therefore do not fulfill the mission of access and opportunity. Valadez (1993, p. 30) writes, "Although community colleges now serve as the principal gateway to higher education for the nation's minority and immigrant populations, they also may be the point of exit for minority students." Additionally, Rendon (1993, p. 8) considers it imperative that a renewed emphasis be placed on the successful transfer of students to universities stating ". . . the real prize is the bachelor's degree; the community college's transfer function is the road to attaining the prize." Rendon (1993) and Katsinas (1994) encourage community colleges to stay on track with the founding mission of democratic ideals and egalitarian notions of equal opportunity by working more closely with students in their transition from the community college to the university. Although not all community college students desire a baccalaureate degree, for those that do, adequate support services must be made available to assist students in attaining that goal.

To further these goals, we propose redefining community colleges as *learning* rather than teaching institutions. Although community colleges have always emphasized teaching over research (Baker, Roueche, and Gillett-Karam, 1990; Bryant, 1994-95), the time has come to heed the admonition that a new learning paradigm is needed. Boggs (1995–96, p. 25) advocates, "the mission should be student learning and we should measure our effectiveness based on student learning." Administrative policies and practices and resources in community colleges must be designed to enhance student learning by focusing on desired learning outcomes.

Student Characteristics and Nature of Involvement in Learning

The mission and subsequent characteristics of community colleges result in critical differences in the involvement of students in their college experience. Indeed, the differences are so great that some community college students do not describe themselves as having a "college experience" at all, but rather "taking classes." And, if current understanding of student involvement (Astin, 1985, 1991; Kuh, Schuh, Whitt, Andreas, Lyons, Strange, Krehbiel, and MacKay; 1991) ideas on "involving colleges" are correct, these students may not be as successful as traditional university students. Even though four-year universities enroll more nontraditional students than ever before, community college students are still more diverse in a variety of ways. This diverse student population results in a considerable challenge for community college educators who want to develop strategies for enhancing student involvement in learning activities.

Academically Disadvantaged Students

For example, the student who is academically disadvantaged selects the community college with its non-competitive admissions by default. Seidman (1993) reports that 11 percent of high school seniors with 'D' averages enter community colleges upon graduation, compared to 1 percent entering senior universities (Seidman, 1993). Almeida (1991) found that many adults entering community colleges read below the college level. And Rendon and Mathews (1989) found that minority high school graduates have lower GPA's and achievement test scores, therefore not qualifying for admission to four-year universities. Bandura's (1986) theory (described in Chapter 2) predicts that these students might have low self-efficacy for college academic work as a result of their low performance in secondary education. When a student has an expectation that effort will not likely pay off in performance, the student is less likely to assign time to learning activities.

Additionally, to be successful at goals beyond developmental education, academically disadvantaged students must be involved in "catching up," prior to or at the same time as pursuing other studies. Bringing skills up to college level first can be discouraging when prolonged and can result in attrition. Taking remedial and college credit courses at the same time places students at a disadvantage in those credit courses that may involve skills beyond their abilities, as well as taking time and energy away from non-remedial courses (Davis and Murrell, 1993). Astin's (1985) and Pace's work (1988) tell us that it is time and effort more than other characteristics that determine success in college and that it is the quantity and quality of involvement that determines whether student learning and personal development occur.Watson and Stage's conceptual framework presented in Chapter 1 is useful in understanding how students' pre-college characteristics and processes (such as quality of effort) affect their personal, social, intellectual, and other development while attending college.

First-Generation College Students. Many community college students are first-generation college students who typically require more academic support and personal guidance than traditional students (Coll, 1995; Pascarella, et al., 1996; Rendon and Mathews, 1989). Although their self-efficacy may have been formed by successful performance in high school, it may also be diminished via observations of family members who did not attend or did not succeed in completing college (Bandura, 1986). Rendon and Mathews (1989) found that in addition to inadequate academic preparation, minority students, many of whom are first-generation college students, often lack an understanding of what is required to be a successful college student as well as the personal skills in motivation or time management. Successful performance is related not only to self-efficacy, but to having basic skills that are essential to performance (Bandura, 1986).

Ethnic Minority Students

Ethnic minorities are more likely to choose community colleges for a variety of reasons. They are more likely to have lower incomes (Rendon, 1993) and so look for a more convenient and affordable learning setting. More than half of Latino college students (O'Brien, 1993) and 43 percent of African-American students are enrolled in community colleges (Otuya, 1994). In 1991, 59 percent of Native American and 4 percent of Asian-Americans who were enrolled in college attended a two-year institution (Western Interstate Commission for Higher Education, as cited by Helfgot and Culp, 1995).

Working College Students. The need to earn one's own income, for whatever reason, has a major impact on time and effort in college (Davis and Murrell, 1993). As many as two-thirds to three-fourths of community college students work, usually off campus (Astin, 1985). Sixty-two percent of the subjects in a study by Smith (1993) worked twenty-one hours or more per week. Smith's findings revealed a strong relationship between students' perceptions that work negatively affected their performance and the amount of time they actually worked. And when students must work, they are often forced to attend college only part-time or at night. Smith (1993) found that attending only at night negatively affected performance as measured by course completion. Thus the time and energy that working and part-time students have available to commit to learning activities is decreased. The challenge for community colleges is to turn this into an asset. Constructivist theory (Phillips, 1995) maintains that learners construct knowledge in specific contexts. Thus students working in fields related to their course of study could actually have an advantage if faculty, administrators, and employers can collaborate to provide work settings and learning objectives that match.

Commuter Students and Students Who Are Parents

The critical element of time and energy (Davis and Murrell, 1993) is also delimited for students who commute (Smith, 1993) and those students who are parents. (Friedlander and MacDougall, 1992; Smith, 1993). Most community college students commute to campus (Astin, 1985) and often at considerable distances. More so than men, returning women (Valadez, 1993) are more likely to be affected by combining college and parenting. In addition to time constraints, these students may experience the negative effect of conflicts between these roles. Valadez (1993) and Helfgot and Culp (1995) note that not all returning women students find cooperation and support at home for child care and household tasks. And for some, academic efforts are sabotaged by other family members. Single parents may face even greater demands on time, as well as role conflicts and emotional pressure to do it all and do it well. Social constructivist self-development theory explains that many women, especially single parents, have independence schemas that obstruct their ability to seek help or support in that they fear depending on others, even in situations where no one could possibly manage competently alone (McCann and Pearlman, 1990).

Students with Special Challenges

Often students with special challenges attend community colleges. Community colleges are more frequently the choice for persons with mental illness (Amada, 1994) or disabilities (Boggs, 1995–96; Henderson, 1995). Other nontraditional students begin or return to college in response to a major life transition, such as the death of a spouse, loss of a job, or the leave-taking of older children. The community college is an option also chosen by homeless individuals, now older teenage-runaways, and battered women. Accompanying such circumstances and life transitions are issues and tasks that drain time, energy, and emotional reserves. Students who have faced severe personal hardships may develop low self-efficacy (Stage, 1996) or have constructed schemas of self and the world that impair fulfilling their needs in the areas of esteem, independence, and power (McCann and Pearlman, 1990)—all of which may negatively impact their learning and their motivation for involvement in learning activities.

Adult Learners. In addition to insufficient time or inadequate academic and/or personal skills, involvement may be affected by expectations. Adult learners (Cross, 1981; Schell and Rojewski, 1995) possess many years of life experience to be integrated with new learning and often individually-defined goals that may or may not align with those of the instructor's. Adult students are less tolerant of learning that has little authentic or practical application and show greater interest in interaction with staff and faculty, as well as student organizations related to their major (Schell and Rojewski, 1995; Whitt, 1994). Consequently, student and faculty expectations may be mismatched, decreasing motivation to be involved in learning activities.

Emotional Involvement

Equally important to learning is the student's place of emotional involvement. According to Astin (1985, 1991), Kuh, et al., (1991) and Pace (1984, 1988) describe "involving colleges" as environments that create a certain learning culture and breed student loyalty to the college. In actuality, some community college students may identify less with the community college they are enrolled in, and more with the university they wish to transfer to or college or high school they are concurrently attending. Those students who were denied admission or dismissed by their preferred university may be ashamed at what they perceive as their inadequacy in having to attend a community college, even pretending to their friends that they are enrolled at a university. The experience of shame or even anticipation of shame results in efforts to ward it off, not the least of which results in maintaining a mask of adequacy to self and others and therefore not seeking help when help is needed. Avoiding shame by not asking for help decreases discomfort even though failure may be the end result.

As is evident, community college students have diverse needs and life activities as they strive to meet everyday responsibilities. However, as Tinto and Russo (1994) maintain, it is possible to enhance student involvement and achievement even in settings where such involvement is not easily acquired. As community college student affairs professionals and faculty, we are challenged to create learning environments that will motivate these students to relate what they are learning in and out of college classrooms to their real-world life goals and ambitions.

Institutional Characteristics That Affect Student Involvement and Learning

Just as students bring to the community college factors which inhibit their motivation for learning, there are institutional factors, perhaps unintentional, that can hinder student involvement and learning. Removing or reducing problems associated with the structure of the institution, instructional faculty, student affairs, and the administration is as important as designing innovative programs for learning to occur.

Lower Division Coursework

Though by design, the less advanced nature of lower division course work, compared to upper division courses at universities, sets limitations on community college student involvement. A student's developmental stage of learning and knowing (King and Baxter Magolda, 1996), as well as a student's novice or expert degree of knowledge attainment in a discipline (Weinstein and Stone, 1993) affect learning differentially. A student in an introductory psychology course for example, does not have the same level of knowledge acquisition and complex organization of that knowledge compared to a senior psychology major. The senior's ability to retrieve knowledge from long-term memory and reorganize it with new learning more closely approximates that of an expert rather than a novice in the field (Weinstein and Stone, 1993). The senior would also possess a higher degree of self-authorship and personal authority, lending facility to his or her motivation and continued learning (King and Baxter Magolda, 1996). In addition to upper-division and graduate courses that capitalize on earlier student learning from lower division courses, their mere existence enhances the institution's learning culture that Kuh et al., (1991) identified as a major element in student involvement.

Job Skills Training

On the other hand, community college vocational, continuing education programs, and apprenticeships with a focus on job skills training have great potential for creating the realistic contexts for learning expounded by social constructivist theory (see Chapter 2; King and Baxter Magolda, 1996; Phillips, 1995). Also, the large number of adjunct faculty who are employed in their respective fields in the community can provide real-world expertise in the classroom (Avakian, 1995). And the many adult workers returning to college to upgrade work-related skills bring with them greater capital from which to make meaning of their new learning (King and Baxter Magolda, 1996). In fact, these students' greater sense of personal authority could be an asset when acknowledged and utilized by faculty.

Instructional Strategies

Increasingly, traditional teaching methods, such as lecture and objective exams, are being questioned as appropriate instructional strategies for assessing or educating nontraditional students (Astin, 1991; Valadez, 1993). Astin (1991, p. 138) suggests that a "cooperative learning model" where "students work on joint projects and learn how to work together toward common goals" is more desirable and facilitates development of teamwork skills. Kempner (1990) notes that well-intentioned faculty can be derailed by a reluctance, although understandable, to define for each other what constitutes excellence in the classroom. Kempner describes a "lack of norms or directions for faculty" and further charges that "faculty accountability, lack of administrative awareness or support, poor leadership, and the organizational climate [are] major hindrances to learning" (p. 220).

Community college professionals can adopt an alternate view of learning that shifts the goal of instruction away from dispensing knowledge and content mastery to assisting learners in applying and adapting knowledge in order to solve real-world problems (Schell and Rojewski, 1995). Adult learners are particularly motivated when they are involved in tasks that directly relate to their personal goals and gain skills that apply to other aspects of their lives (Cross, 1981; Stage, 1996; Wlodkowski, 1993). In this way, faculty encourage students to apply skills learned in class to identify possible solutions to challenges faced in out-of-class settings—home, job, or community.

Freire's theory of conscientization (1970/1993) advocates a teacher-student learning partnership that uses dialogue (authentic communication) to stimulate critical thinking that results in increased consciousness. Freire argues against the "banking concept" of education in which "the scope of action allowed the students extends only as far as receiving, feeling, and storing the deposits" (p. 53). Freire developed the theory of conscientization to respond to the learning needs of the politically and socially oppressed illiterate people in Latin America. However, his principles have practical implications in community colleges in educating traditionally disfranchised groups, who often experience economic and social oppression and perceive they have no control over their circumstances.

Faculty Interaction

Some faculty exhibit attitudes that inhibit student involvement. Entwistle (1992) cites faculty misunderstanding of students' varying educational orientations as a source of student dissatisfaction. He notes that students often have an implied contract regarding what they want from a course and this may be more important to them than even the course requirements. Long and Walsh (1993, p. 162–163) suggest ". . . students will be more successful in classes that among other things give them the opportunity to be involved in self diagnosing their learning needs and planning the course " (p. 162–163). Valadez (1993) notes that community college faculty are sometimes paternalistic toward the very developmental students the college purports to serve, thus opposing conscientization, social constructivist, and self-efficacy theories which promote respect for the learner's state of knowing and support his or her evolving stage of learning and self-confidence as a knower (Bandura, 1986; Freire, 1970/1993; King and Baxter Magolda, 1996). For example, Lundeberg and Moch (1995) advise that faculty stop asking "what's wrong with women that they don't like science?" and start asking "what's wrong with the teaching of science that women don't like it?" (p. 312–313). Their interviews indicated that women students attributed their most valuable learning to occurrences *outside* the classroom because their preferred "connected knowing" learning style was constrained by the typical way science was taught in the classroom.

Additionally, isolation of community college faculty with each other, students, and university colleagues is pinpointed by a number of researchers. Kempner (1990) found "instructors doing their own thing and [having] very little contact with each other" (p. 225). And Rendon and Mathews (1989, p. 320) report a low level of faculty involvement in student orientation, academic advising, or transfer articulation with four-year university faculty.

Freidlander and McDougall (1992) note that students' personal growth, satisfaction with college, and persistence would be increased with greater interaction with instructors. Stage and Muller emphasize in Chapter 2 the importance of faculty dialogue with students so as to facilitate the student's knowledge construction of a given discipline's content. Students benefit when faculty directly relate this content to students' lives outside the classroom and not just abstract theory.

The Role of Counselors in Learning

Helfgot and Culp (1995) and Coll (1995) discuss the role of counselors in community colleges in helping students clarify educational and career goals and in providing support for students with academic and personal problems. Pineda and Bowes (1995) recognize that this central role is crucial to the overall objectives of the community college. Unlike student affairs at four-year universities which maintain separate programs for counseling students with academic concerns, career planning, and personal problems, such functions at community colleges are performed by the same student development personnel (Coll, 1995). This organization lends itself well to integrating student learning and development. Integration allows for easier utilization of concepts of conscientization (Freire, 1970/ 1993), constructivism (King and Baxter Magolda, 1996; Phillips, 1995), and other learning theories. However, even with the advantage of greater organizational integration, the community college counselors' role may need to be broadened to adequately address the needs of the college's changing and increasingly disfranchised population. The following are proactive actions counselors can take:

Increase their Awareness of Special Counseling Needs of Ethnic Minority Students and Use Multiculturally Relevant Career Guidance Materials

Watson and Stage in Chapter 1 and Valadez (1993) advocate that nontraditional students' "cultural capital" be valued and integrated in their learning experiences. Counselors can become proactive in providing services since ethnic minority and other nontraditional students often terminate counseling prematurely or do not pursue counseling at all. Counselors and other student affairs professionals (e.g., academic advisors and student development specialists) might heed the words of a colleague, "We make the best of each contact we have with a student because it may be the *only* contact." (Whitt, 1994, p. 317).

Practice More Intrusive Advising and Proactive Counseling

Coll (1995) and Rendon (1993) identified the need for counselors to intervene with nontraditional students by clarifying their educational and career goals. Intrusive advising can include a requirement that all new and continuing students meet with an academic advisor to discuss educational goals and selection of courses. New student orientation and personal development courses or workshops focusing on help-seeking skills, goal setting, stress and time management, study skills, test anxiety, and career decision making that counselors usually offer can be of particular help. Pineda and Bowes (1995) recommend that counselors establish networks that recreate the support of the home community, such as ethnic student organizations or women's support groups.

Understand Relationships Between Financial Assistance and the Safety Net of the Community's Welfare and Social Services Systems

Counselors, even in financial aid offices, often eschew performing social work functions and/or assisting students with financial planning as "not part of my job." To help disfranchised students, this may need to be part of the job!

Learn to Assess Learning Preferences and/or Intervene with Various Student Learning Problems and Learning Disabilities

This would likely necessitate improvement in the quality of knowledge and skills of counselors. Stage (1996) discusses Bandura's (1986) findings that the role of teachers' beliefs in their own instructional efficacy contributed significantly to students' academic achievement.

It may be that counselors in community colleges may also question their own efficacy related to their knowledge of learning and learning problems. Indeed, to what extent have counselors at community colleges or four-year universities received graduate preparation in these areas? Counselors currently in the field might assimilate the hallmarks of a learning organization to help determine best practice for their role, goals, and services to students (Boggs, 1995-1996; Entwistle, 1992).

Perform a More Direct Role in Students' Knowledge Construction

Counselors can facilitate learning by recognizing students who have low self-efficacy (Bandura, 1986), an external locus of control, and/or a limited awareness of their socio-cultural situation (Freire, 1970/1993). Counselor understanding of conscientization theory could assist students in developing an internal locus of control by questioning their socio-cultural reality as suggested by Stage and Muller in Chapter 2. Through meaningful dialogue with disfranchised students about their realities, counselors and other student affairs professionals can help students recognize that their state of being is not fated and unalterable, but merely limiting. Through inquiry, reflection, and a deepening consciousness of their situation, students can be involved in transforming their reality. Through this process of inquiry and transformation using students' personal experiences students can begin to feel in control, to create their new socio-cultural reality, and to perceive themselves as capable of solving problems and thinking critically.

Develop Expert Knowledge of Self-Efficacy Theory

With so many community college students having academically disadvantaged backgrounds and prior negative educational experiences, low self-efficacy is a major impediment to their retention and accomplishment of their educational goals. Coll (1995) also found an increase over the years in the severity of student problems such as poor study habits, lack of time management skills, inadequate academic skills, poor organizing and prioritizing skills, and anxiety, as perceived by community college counselors. Brackney and Karabenick (1995) recommend that even students who are in emotional distress can be helped most by counselors focusing on academic self-efficacy, study skills, and help-seeking skills. Counselors could also offer opportunities for students with low self-efficacy to get together with students who have successfully completed their goals at the community college or who are now succeeding at their transfer university.

The Role of Other Student Affairs Professionals in Learning

Student Affairs professionals other than counselors can play a vital role in student learning as well. Community colleges could benefit from encouraging every student affairs professional who has contact with students to develop co-curricular learning experiences for students.

Facilitate the Integration of In-class and Out-of-class Activities

The linking of students to cultural activities and public service agencies is recommended through institutional efforts and resources (Astin, 1991; Kuh et al, 1991; Pascarella et al, 1996). "Extracurricular" major-related student organizations could become co-curricular by integrating course objectives into the activities of the organization and by faculty requiring participation for partial course credit or as lab credit. Smith (1993) found that in addition to time spent studying, hours per week spent on campus other than class time were important environmental variables affecting student progress. Nontraditional students may particularly benefit from this approach. Rendon and Mathews (1989) found that few ethnic minorities participated in extracurricular activities. Whitt (1994) found that major-related student organizations are of particular interest to adult students.

Student affairs professionals working in student activities can be instrumental in encouraging nontraditional students to participate in institutional governance, campus clubs and organizations, and volunteer learning experiences. Kuh et al, (1991) found that these are the kinds of out-of-class experiences that contribute to student learning and personal development. These activities allow students to develop effective interpersonal skills, communication skills, decision-making skills, consensus-building skills, and other learning that enhances community college students' educational experiences. It is important that student activities officers provide leadership training for students and demonstrate to students the value of co-curricular experiences to their overall learning in college. An added bonus that community colleges can provide is a leadership "transcript" that includes the various co-curricular activities of students, which students can use as evidence of their participation in these learning experiences. Student activities officers could also help student leaders understand the importance of accessing other services, such as counseling and advising, whenever such services could enhance their learning.

Help Students Find Adequate Financial Resources

Lack of resources is a significant barrier for many students (Seidman, 1995). Although traditionally seen as mere processors of financial assistance, the role of Financial Aid specialists could also be expanded to play a broader role in students' learning. Financial Aid Offices could also expand their mandated loan counseling to comprehensive financial planning for students, including budgeting and debt management.

Smith's (1993) finding of a strong relationship between amount of time students actually worked and their perception that work negatively affected school performance leads to the possibility that to help students learn, colleges need to support students' working less. Extensive current databases of local and non-local student aid could be developed for student use on campus in Financial Aid offices. Colleges can pursue collaborations with community employers to offer tuition or textbook cost reimbursement and scholarships to their employees—not just to those whose educational goals align with their job responsibilities, but to all employees as a service to the community. These expectations can be made part of governments giving tax abatements when recruiting new companies. Colleges can give public recognition and awards to those employers who give release time for class attendance by employees who are also students.

Facilitate the Use of Community College Students in Peer-Helping, Paid Positions

Students can be employed as recruitment "ambassadors", peer orientation advisors, peer academic advisors, tutors, learning assistants for students with disabilities, assessment testing monitors, teaching, research, and lab assistants, graders, study session leaders, and in a number of other roles. Friedlander and MacDougall (1992) suggest that on-campus jobs related to students' fields of study, especially student peer teaching and research assistantships (in some community colleges), provide increased contacts with faculty and peers, which promote students' involvement in learning activities and satisfaction with college. Federal work-study money, as well as other institutional hourly monies, can be used to fund these positions. These types of on-campus jobs are beneficial financially to nontraditional students and at the same time help students become socially integrated into the college, which contributes to their retention. Student affairs professionals and faculty employing students in these diverse roles can help students understand the learning value of these peer-helping positions. Success in these jobs can help build student self-esteem, which may contribute to increased motivation for other learning experiences.

The Role of Administrators in Learning

Academic administrators can provide an environment in which counselors, other student affairs professionals, and faculty are encouraged to be learners and seek personal mastery that will benefit students.

Be More Objective in Evaluating your Roles in Benefiting Student Learning

Unfortunately, administrators may abdicate leadership for student involvement through their own unquestioned assumptions. Tinto and Russo (1994) suggest that college leadership has pointed the finger at student behaviors and obligations long enough and that "we should more carefully consider the character of our own obligations to construct the sorts of educational settings in which students will *want* to become involved" (p. 24). Paternalistic attitudes of knowing what is best for the student excludes students from involvement in the very decisions that determine whether and what they learn.

Value and Assess Learning Outcomes

Rendon and Mathews (1989) advise that administration implement institutional research on retention, transfer, and achievement and use it in planning and decision-making. Boggs (1995-1996) asserts that institutions have too long focused on measurement of their productivity in terms of cost per hour of instruction, rather than their contributions to student learning. In Chapter 8 Lee Upcraft provides a framework employing the model presented by Stage and Watson for assessing student learning. Administrators with a focus on decreasing costs either increase class size or faculty teaching loads, both of which may have a negative effect on student learning.

Organize the Institution Toward Student Learning

Rendon (1993) found that where administration structured the institution to enhance certain functions, such as transfer, students showed higher rates of transfer. Rendon and Mathews (1989) advise that the administration create articulation agreements with universities and provide adequate transfer information in catalogs. For example, community college administrators can request that their faculty be placed on four-year universities' curriculum committees, as well as invite their faculty to sit on curriculum committees of the community college. It is the role of the administration to successfully negotiate with reluctant university officials, as well as its own reluctant faculty and staff, to bring about needed changes. Making change systematically and on a large scale critically depends on the expressed interest in and informed actions of the community college administration.

Devise Policies and Practices that Lead Student Affairs Professionals, Faculty, Administrators, and Others to Focus on Desired Learning Outcomes for Students

An organizational climate can be created wherein community colleges facilitate inquiry on varied views about student learning, a personal commitment among educators to learn and improve, and a recognition of our interconnectedness through underlying structures. It is within such a climate that institutional factors which hinder student involvement and learning can be more successfully examined.

Community College Partnerships
to Promote Learning

Community colleges have enormous potential to create learning organizations (Senge, 1990) in which there is a genuine interest in what matters to students and a willingness to use a systems approach to problem solving. Entwistle (1992) maintains that a systems analysis, both at the departmental and institutional level, will be required "if the overall quality of student learning in higher education is to be substantially improved" (p. 1738). Administration can support student involvement in college by distributing institutional resources to programs and new initiatives that facilitate student learning and personal development and assessment of learning outcomes. We need to ". . . view student learning and student needs through new lenses" (Cross, 1996, p.11), engage in professional inquiry—"talking and thinking about information on student learning on our own campuses" (p. 7), and set aside "turfs and specialties that have divided campuses for years" (p. 8).

Creating Seamless Learning Environments

Seamless learning environments can be created by academic and student affairs units working as partners to engage in systems thinking and to develop personal mastery that will lead community colleges to evolve as learning organizations. Senge (1990) describes learning organizations as those "capable of continually monitoring, modifying, enhancing, or abandoning existing programs; creating new services to meet customer needs; questioning assumptions and values, not just the strategies used to reach specific goals; and searching for gaps that exist between vision and values and day-to-day actions" (Helfgot and Culp, 1995, p. 45). In such seamless environments, the cognitive and affective dimensions are viewed by student affairs, faculty, and administrators as parts of one process—"knowledge construction, meaning making, and awareness of self are presumed to be integrated within the developing human being" (King and Baxter Magolda, 1996, p.163).

Student affairs professionals and faculty can partner to help students recognize that their learning in the classroom is related to their out-of-class lives. Increased time in dialogue with students about what and how they are learning (Whitt, 1994), as well as guiding students in drawing connections, integrating, and applying what they are learning in class to their real-world lives (Schroeder and Hurst, 1996) are avenues for increasing involvement. Institutional rewards systems can be designed to recognize faculty for involvement with students in out-of-class activities, as well as student affairs professionals for providing meaningful out-of-class learning experiences that assist students in developing critical thinking, leadership, and other skills.

Student affairs professionals and faculty can also be rewarded for working collaboratively to create learning contexts that students view as meaningful. Stage and Muller note in Chapter 2 that student affairs professionals can work with faculty and academic administrators as *context setters* to provide "experiences that give structure and meaning to classroom learning for college students."

Summary

Community college students provide a challenge to Astin's (1985) involvement theory since their commuter lives are already full of obligations outside college (Tinto and Russo 1994). The challenge for student affairs professionals is to work collaboratively with faculty to understand the character of community college student involvement, to reward involvement in learning activities that naturally occur outside of class, and to provide co-curricular experiences that utilize learners' out of class experiences to enrich their in-class learning, and vice versa. Kuh, Vesper, and Krehbiel (1994) recommend that faculty encourage and give credit to students for utilizing the resources of the campus (e.g., library, learning centers, co-curricular activities such as plays, art exhibits, study skills workshops) and resources of the community (e.g., employment opportunities, internships, volunteerism, and music, art, and theater options). Muller and Stage, in Chapter 6 discuss service learning that can capitalize on community college students' community and public service, creating intentional learning contexts.

Student affairs professionals have found Pace's (1984) Community College Student Experience Questionnaire (CCSEQ) useful in identifying the learning activities that are important to student achievement (Davis and Murrell, 1993), and therefore to the creation of seamless learning environments. Friedlander and MacDougall (1992) discuss studies using the CCSEQ which found that the greater the level of student involvement in learning opportunities, the greater the progress students made in achieving their educational goals. Learning activities studied included course-related activities; use of the library; contacts with faculty, counselors, and other students; activities related to art, athletics, music, science, theater, writing; and campus clubs and organizations. These findings suggest the co-curricular activities that could be developed for students through partnerships between student affairs professionals, faculty, and others at the college and in the wider community.

Smith (1993) found in using the CCSEQ in his study of community college students that three quality of effort variables made contributions to course completion: library activities, counseling, and participation in art, music, and theater activities. Smith (1993, p. 116) noted that "making an appointment with a counselor to discuss transfer" emerged as the significant contributor to unit completion. Smith (1993, p. 116) recommends that "a specific intervention regarding transfer counseling might improve persistence, particularly for students with a higher number of semesters completed at the community college." He determined that the more semesters students are enrolled at the community college, the less likely they are to seek counseling services. This finding is instructive given the need to encourage more underrepresented students to persist in college and successfully transfer to four-year universities. Counselors could design more systematic and coordinated interventions for students that address academic and personal concerns about transfer; could remain knowledgeable about transfer courses and policies and partner with area universities and colleges to ensure a smooth transfer for students; could collaborate with faculty in making transfer options known to students; and could make themselves more accessible (Bauer and Bauer, 1994; Pineda and Bowes, 1995; Rendon and Mathews, 1989).

Student affairs professionals could promote enrichment programs for themselves and faculty which emphasize teaching practices and strategies including diverse teaching styles that are more successful with nontraditional students. They can encourage faculty and each other to gain personal mastery of learning styles, multicultural and other special needs, and evaluation of learning problems in order to better understand the learning needs of its diverse population. Counselors could be provided with incentives to acquire skills in multicultural counseling and "to intervene at the institutional level on behalf of minority group members" (Pineda and Bowes, 1995, p. 154).

Student affairs professionals can assist faculty in recognizing when student learning is at risk and collaborate with both students and faculty by designing action plans that promote success such as those exemplified in Chapter 2. We can make faculty and students aware of support services; and clarify the referral process to these services (Entwistle, 1992; Wlodkowksi, 1993). Wlodkowski writes, "Because adults have so many crucial responsibilities outside of the learning environment (family, job, and community), the emotions that result from problems due to these obligations may impinge on their motivation during learning" (p. 184). Student affairs professionals can advocate learning contexts that have proven successful in integrating in-class and out-of-class learning such as coordinated studies programs, similar to freshman interest groups (FIGS) at four-year universities (Schroeder and Hurst, 1996).

Tinto and Russo (1994) describe a coordinated studies program which created a learning environment in a community college that promoted student involvement and achievement. Students registered for a common set of thematically linked courses (e.g., Conflict in America or Women in the 21st Century) taught by two to four faculty members from varying academic disciplines. Students in the program were given a voice in the construction of their knowledge by "...thinking across disciplines, exploring key concepts in depth, and relating course materials to their own experiences" (p. 23). Participants reported greater involvement in academic and social activities and greater developmental gains than students in the regular curriculum. The coordinated studies program provided students with a "knowable group of fellow students with whom early friendships were formed" (p. 21). This community of peers provided support to each other in class and out of class.

Special programs designed to address specific learning needs can be offered. Becherer and Becherer (1995) discuss a number of exemplary student affairs programs at over fifty-three community colleges that are designed to enhance student learning, persistence, and success. They describe freshman seminars, personal growth and success classes for women or minority students, leadership development programs, adaptive computer technology and cooperative education programs for students with disabilities, student peer ambassador programs, automated orientation, financial support for co-curriculum programs . . ." (p. 71–72). Creative ways of assessing these programs are provided as well.

Conclusions

Community colleges continue to be in a unique position to provide access and opportunity for higher learning to underrepresented, disfranchised groups but can devise a new learning paradigm to achieve their full potential. A reexamination of the role and mission of community colleges is recommended so that learning truly becomes the primary purpose of these institutions. A greater emphasis on the learning needs of a diverse student population and a renewed interest in the transfer role to fulfill the mission of access and opportunity are recommended, as well as strengthening and expanding partnerships. Increased resources and enhanced learning contexts gained through community partnerships are vital in preparing new students entering the colleges' open doors to function in a technological environment.

References

Almeida, D. A. (1991). Do underprepared students and those with lower academic skills belong in the community college? A question of policy in light of the "mission." *Community College Review, 18*, (4), 28–32.

Amada, G. (1994). The role of the college mental health program. In D. D. Gehring (Series Ed.) and D. P. Young (Ed.), *Coping with the disruptive college student: A practical model.* (pp. 51–63). Asheville, NC: College Administration Publications.

Astin, A. W. (1985). *Achieving Educational Excellence*, San Francisco: Jossey-Bass.

Astin, A. W. (1991). The changing American college student: Implications for educational policy and practice. *Higher Education, 22*, 129-143.

Avakian, A. N. (1995). Conflicting demands for adjunct faculty. *Community College Journal, 65*, (6), 34–36.

Baker, G. A., Roueche, J. E., and Gillett-Karam, R. (1990). *Teaching as leading: Profiles of excellence in the open-door college.* Washington, D.C.: The American Association of Community and Junior Colleges.

Bandura, A. (1986). *Social foundations of thought and action: A social-cognitive theory.* Englewood Cliffs, N.J.: Prentice-Hall. 390–453.

Bauer, P. F. and Bauer, K. W. (1994, Summer). The community college as an academic bridge: Academic and personal concerns of community college students before and after transferring to a four-year institution. *College and University, LXIX*, (3), 116–122.

Becherer, J. J. and Becherer, J. H. (1995, Spring). Programs, services, and activities: A survey of the community college landscape. In S. R. Helfgot and M. M. Culp (Eds.), *New directions for student services:*

Promoting student success in the community college, (69), San Francisco: Jossey-Bass.

Boggs, G. R. (1995–96). The learning paradigm. *Community College Journal, 66*, (3), 24–27.

Brackney, B. E. and Karabenick, S. A. (1995). Psychopathology and academic performance: The role of motivation and learning strategies. *Journal of Counseling Psychology, 42*, (4), 456–465.

Bryant, D. W. (1994-1995). The battle of instructional effectiveness. *Community College Journal, 65*, (3), 16–22.

Cohen, A. M. and Brawer, F. B. (1989). *The American community college*. San Francisco: Jossey-Bass.

Coll, K. M. (1995). Career, personal, and educational problems of community college students: Severity and frequency. *NASPA Journal, 32* (4), 270–278.

Cross, K. P. (1981). *Adults as learners; Increasing participation and facilitating learning*. San Francisco: Jossey-Bass.

Cross, K. P. (1996). New lenses on learning. *On Campus, 1*, (1), 4–9.

Davis, T. M. and Murrell, P. H. (1993). *Turning teaching into learning: The role of student responsibility in the collegiate experience*. ASHE-ERIC Higher Education Report No. 8. Washington, D.C.: The George Washington University, School of Education and Human Development.

Driver, R., Asoko, H., Leach, J., Mortimer, E., and Scott, P. (1994). Constructing scientific knowledge in the classroom. *Educational Researcher, 23*(7), 5–12.

Entwistle, N. (1992). Student learning and study strategies. In B.R. Clark and G. Neave (Eds.), *Encyclopedia of higher education, 3*, 1730–1740. New York: Praeger.

Freire, P. (1970/1993). *Pedagogy of the oppressed*, New York: Continuum Publishing.

Friedlander, J. and MacDougall, P. (1992). Achieving student success through student involvement. *Community College Review, 20*, (1), 20–28.

Helfgot, S. R. and Culp, M. M. (1995). Promoting student success in the community college. In S. R. Helfgot and M. M. Culp (Eds.), *New directions for student services: Promoting student success in the community college*, (69), San Francisco: Jossey-Bass.

Henderson, C. (1995). Postsecondary students with disabilities: Where are they enrolled? *Research Briefs, 6*, (6).

Katsinas, S. G. (1994). Is the open door closing? The democratizing role of the community college in the post-cold war era. *Community College Journal, 64*, (5), 22–28.

Kempner, K. (1990). Faculty culture in the community college: Facilitating or hindering learning? *The Review of Higher Education, 13*, (2), 215–235.

King, P. M. and Baxter Magolda, M .B. (1996). A developmental perspective on learning. *Journal of College Student Development, 37*, (2). 163–173.

Kuh, G. D., Schuh, J. H., Whitt, E. J., Andreas, R. E., Lyons, J. W., Strange, C. C., Krehbiel, L. E., and Mackay, K. A. (1991). *Involving colleges.* San Francisco: Jossey-Bass.

Kuh, G. D., Vesper, N. and Krehbiel, L .E. (1994). Student learning at metropolitan universities. *Higher Education: Handbook of Theory and Research, X.* Agathon Press.

Lazar, A. M. (1995). Who is studying in groups and why? Peer collaboration outside the classroom. *College Teaching, 43*, (2), 61–65.

Long, H.B. and Walsh, S.M. (1993). Self-directed learning research in the community/junior college: Description, conclusions and recommendations. *Community College Journal of Research and Practice, 17*, 153–166.

Lundeberg, M. A. and Moch, S. D. (1995). Influence of social interaction on cognition. *Journal of Higher Education, 66*, (3), 312–335.

McCann, I. L. and Pearlman, L. A. (1990). *Psychological trauma adult survivor: Theory, therapy, and transformation*, New York: Brunner/Mazel. 12–27, 280–306.

O'Brien, E. M. (1993). Latinos in higher education. *Research Briefs, 4*, (4).

Otuya, E. (1994). African Americans in higher education. *Research Briefs, 5*, (3).

Pace, C. R. (1984). *Measuring the quality of college students experiences.* University of California, Los Angeles: Higher Education Research Institute.

Pace, C. R. (1988). *CSEQ: Test manual and norms.* University of California, Los Angeles: Center for the study of evaluation.

Pascarella, E. T., Edison, M., Whitt, E., Hagedorn, L. S., Nora, A., and Terenzini, P. T. (1996). What have we learned from the first year of the National Study of Student Learning? *Journal of College Student Development, 37,* (2), 182–192.

Phillips, D. C. (1995). The good, the bad and the ugly: The many faces of constructivism. *Educational Researcher, 24* (7), 5–12.

Pierce, D. R. (1996). What you need to know about two-year colleges. *Peterson's Guide to Two-Year Colleges.* New Jersey: Peterson's Guides.

Pineda, E. N. and Bowes, G. (1995). Multicultural campuses: The challenge for community college counselors. *Community College Journal of Research and Practice, 19,* 151–160.

Rendon, L. I. (1993). Eyes on the prize: Students of color and the bachelor's degree. *Community College Review, 21,* (3), 3–13.

Rendon, L. I. and Matthews, T. B. (1989). Success of community college students: Current issues. *Education and Urban Society, 21,* (3), 312–327.

Schell, J. W. and Rojewski, J. W. (1995). Community and technical college teaching for thoughtful results. *Community College Journal of Research and Practice, 19,* 133–150.

Schroeder, C. C. and Hurst, J. C. (1996). Designing learning environments that integrate curricular and cocurricular experiences. *Journal of College Student Development, 37,* (2), 174–181.

Seidman, A. (1993). Needed: A research methodology to assess community college effectiveness. *American Association of Community Colleges Journal, 63,* (5), 36–40.

Seidman, A. (1995). The community college: A challenge for change. *Community College Journal of Research and Practice, 19,* 247–254.

Senge, P. M. (1990). *The fifth discipline.* New York: Doubleday.

Smith, B. M. (1993). The effect of quality of effort on persistence among traditional-aged community college students. *Community College Journal of Research and Practice, 17,* 103–122.

Stage, F. K. (1996). Setting the context: Psychological theories of learning. *Journal of College Student Development, 37,* 2, 227–235.

Tinto, V. and Russo, P. (1994). Coordinated studies programs: Their effect on student involvement at a community college. *Community College Review, 22,* (2), 16–25.

Valadez, J. (1993). Cultural capital and its impact on the aspirations of nontraditional community college students. *Community College Review, 21*, (3), 30–43.

Weinstein, C. E. and Stone, G. V. M. (1993). Broadening our conception of general education: The self-regulated learner. In Raisman, N. A. (Ed.). *Directing general education outcomes: Vol. 81. New Directions for Community Colleges, 21*, (1), (pp. 31–39). San Francisco: Jossey-Bass.

Whitt, E. J. (1994). Encouraging adult learner involvement. *NASPA Journal, 31*, (4), 309–318.

Wlodkowski, R. J. (1993). *Enhancing adult motivation to learn.* San Francisco: Jossey-Bass.

6

Service-Learning: Exemplifying the Connections between Theory and Practice

Patricia Muller
Frances K. Stage

Service-learning exemplifies the connections between theory and practice, and provides an excellent example of a holistic systems approach that closely links academic and student affairs professionals. This chapter focuses on the application of the previously described learning theories (Chapter 2) to service-learning, a very specific student affairs venue that is of growing interest on college campuses. Additionally, service-learning can be an important supplement to the educational process as described in Chapter 1.

Service-learning is the integration of community and public service with structured and intentional learning goals (Kendall and Associates, 1990; Stanton, 1990; Zlotkowski, 1996). Service-learning initiatives allow faculty and student affairs professionals to collaboratively engage students in an educational process that maximizes student learning and personal development. Service-learning programs

encourage natural partnerships between institutions of higher education and the community, providing students with experiences that
combine real community needs with intentional learning goals, con-
scious reflection, and critical analysis.   By focusing on theories related to learning, student affairs professionals can more fully
describe the symbiotic relationship that exists between formal classroom learning and out-of-class learning opportunities. Additionally,
we can create an increasingly seamless educational process that fosters student learning, involvement and gains.

This chapter provides background information on service-learning. An application of four learning theories to service-learning will
follow: (1) social-constructivism, (2) Kolb's learning cycle, (3) self-
efficacy, and (4) Freire's conscientization. Case studies are used to
illustrate the link between the theories and service. Discussion and a
conclusion follow.

Background

Volunteer organizations, and centers that coordinate community service activities and/or pair students with local agencies, have existed
on many college campuses during the cyclical surges of interest in
volunteerism throughout the past four decades (Kendall and Associates, 1990). The current service movement began to gain momentum
in the late 1980s, and during the 1990s higher education has increasingly focused on more integrally linking service to the academic
curriculum. The term "service-learning" emphasizes this integration
of service and learning, and is increasingly evident on college campuses where service is being directly coupled with academic courses
and classroom learning (Markus, Howard and King, 1993).

Reframing service not as a supplement to the formal curriculum
but as a necessary component of student learning explicitly linked to
academic growth distinguishes service-learning from previous volunteer movements. Although the basic principles of service-learning are
rooted in the works of educators such as Dewey (1916) and Tyler
(1949), service-learning differs from traditional experiential learning
(Seigel and Rockwood, 1993). Experiential learning opportunities (i.e.,
internships, co-op programs, practica, clinicals, field experiences, student teaching) focus on extending students' professional skills, whereas service-learning engages students in organized service activities
designed to meet identified community needs while also enhancing
students' skills and understanding of course content (Bringle and
Hatcher, 1996).

Higher education has long recognized the contribution of community service to the development of students' civic and moral responsibility, but these benefits have not been considered central to the academic mission of the institution. Consequently, community service activities have traditionally been relegated to student affairs divisions while experiential learning programs have remained under the domain of academic affairs. However, both student affairs professionals and faculty are now beginning to recognize the potential for service-learning to provide the type of holistic systems approach described in Chapter 1.

During the 1990s, student affairs professionals acknowledged that learning from volunteer activities is not automatic (Kendall and Associates, 1990). The student who spends three hours a week serving meals to the homeless, mentoring at-risk youth, or building homes for low-income families, returns to the residence hall, perhaps having "enjoyed" the volunteer work and feeling a sense of satisfaction from the altruistic experience, but not necessarily engaging in critical thinking about the existence of poverty, oppression or homelessness (Rhoads, 1997).

Even within student affairs, the notion of reflection and learning coupled with service is not new (Schine, 1995). However, learning frequently seems to be forgotten, or at least assumed to happen while more concrete aspects of the volunteerism (e.g., agency placement, quantifying student service, recruiting volunteers) occupy program directors' concerns. Additionally, experiences often promote a power imbalance of the privileged "haves" providing for the "have-nots" (Radest, 1993; Schine, 1995). Frequently, community service exposes students to those "less fortunate" without engaging students in learning processes that increase understanding of the context of the social problems (e.g., causes of poverty and racism, plight of the elderly) they encounter. To address these issues, student affairs professionals view service-learning as a viable means of reemphasizing student learning and personal development in higher education by intentionally designing service models that promote learning and cognitive development. Faculty also increasingly recognize that intentionally combining service and learning offers great potential for helping students attain higher levels of learning and cognitive development. Service-learning is viewed as an additional *means* for reaching educational objectives (Bringle and Hatcher, 1996), including the cognitive development of students. Additionally, faculty are beginning to recognize that service-learning maximizes the pedagogical advantages of experiential learning (Markus, Howard and King, 1993).

In the last five years, knowledge regarding service-learning practices has profereated. Jacoby and Associates (1996) specifically discuss service-learning in higher education. Kendall and Associates (1990) provide a comprehensive resource for those interested in establishing or strengthening service-learning programs on their campuses. The book delineates factors that distinguish service-learning from community service programs and defines for both academic and student affairs the critical components of service-learning, such as emphasis on reciprocity and the integration of intentional learning goals. Stanton (1990) examines the faculty role in service-learning. Campus Compact provides invaluable support and resources at the state and national level, including Campus Compact's Summer Institute for the Project on Integrating Service and Academic Study. Literature, such as Barber and Battistoni (1993), documents the implementation of service-learning within specific academic disciplines. Rhoads (1997) uses description of community service in four contexts to frame a model of community service and calls for a reformation of higher education toward development of our ethic of caring.

Although much practical advice has been generated on integrating service with academic study, we still lack literature that discusses student and academic affairs' common goals and joint role in engaging students in service-learning. Knowing the connection between theory and practice will help student affairs professionals collaborate with faculty in the integration of service and learning. The first step towards this end is increasing our understanding regarding *how* service-learning enhances students' cognitive development. In Chapter 2, we are reminded that part of our role as members of the student affairs profession might be to reinterpret the contexts within which learning takes place. Service-learning provides an excellent opportunity to directly link the learning activities that occur outside the classroom with the learning that occurs within a classroom context.

Learning Theories Applied to Service-Learning

Discussions of the benefits of service have historically been limited to the socio-developmental domain. The majority of research documents these socio-developmental outcomes within secondary school sponsored service programs (Giles and Eyler, 1994), such as gains in self-esteem (Conrad and Hedin, 1982) and moral development (Hamilton and Fenzel, 1988). By examining college student outcomes, recent research such as Giles and Eyler (1994) has begun to move higher education beyond the anecdotal evidence frequently cited in discussions of service-learning.

However, there are relatively few attempts to define and directly measure the cognitive learning that occurs in higher education service programs. Most studies rely on students' self-reports that they "learned more" than they did in formal classrooms (Giles and Eyler, 1994). Although postsecondary research is increasingly addressing the cognitive development associated with service-learning (see Markus, Howard and King, 1993; and Batchelder and Root, 1994), the discussions have almost exclusively focused on cognitive learning *outcomes*. While the literature has started to focus on the cognitive "output" associated with service-learning, the "process" component of the conceptual framework for student learning, involvement and gains, described in Chapter 1, has been left largely unexamined. We have begun to articulate the "what," but not the "how" of students learning through participation in service-learning.

Given that community service has historically fallen under the domain of student affairs, it is not surprising that at times when the "process" has been explored it has occurred within the realm of student development and cognitive development theories familiar to student affairs professionals. For example, Delve, Mintz and Stewart (1990) describe the application of Kohlberg, Perry, and Gilligan's moral and ethical developmental models to service-learning programs and policies. As described in more general terms in Chapter 2, the tendency to not incorporate psychological learning theories in our efforts to enhance student learning has been paralleled in service-learning initiatives. Utilizing learning theories will allow us to make an intellectual connection that helps academics, graduate students and administrators understand our collaborative role in enhancing student learning through service.

This section explores the relevance of four learning theories to service-learning programs: (1) social-constructivism, (2) Kolb's learning cycle, (3) self-efficacy, and (4) Freire's conscientization. Case studies are utilized for each learning theory to illustrate its relevance to service-learning, and the application of theory to practice. More detailed descriptions of these theories are available in Chapter 2.

Social-Constructivism

Social-constructivism, described in more detail in Chapter 2, is based upon the tenet that knowledge is not transmitted directly from one person to another, but results from a knowledge-construction process that is actively built by the learner (Driver, Asoko, Leach, Mortimer and Scott, 1994). The individual construction of knowledge perspective emphasizes the importance of physical experiences that encourage learners to attempt to understand and interpret phenomena for themselves. Cobb (1994) asserts that both constructivism and social-contructivism stress the crucial role that activity plays in learning, and that enculturation combined with constructivism might best facilitate learning.

Perhaps the reader can most easily relate to the approach to constructivism as applied to high school science classes. In chemistry, students read about acids and bases, become "socialized" into the language of chemists, and solve related mathematical problems. But in addition, once or twice a week, students combine chemicals, observe reactions, and create laboratory reports designed to provide a foundation upon which they 'construct' abstract chemical principles that they learn. Hence the term social constructivism.

Similarly, the nature and characteristics of service-learning programs provide strong opportunities for students to construct, or reconstruct, their own knowledge. Educators can convey theories to students within the classroom that have been constructed by others. The students' learning is then further enhanced when they subjectively learn these same theories, and re-construct their own knowledge through service-learning activities. Consider the following case study:

> Marco Molina, an undergraduate student, is enrolled in a psychology course focused on child development. The professor has been lecturing on Piaget's stages of child development. Marco listens attentively, taking notes and trying to grasp the concepts involved. That night, Marco reads the chapter from the course text that covers Piaget. He memorizes the stages, but beyond the ability to repeat them back "word for word" for the purposes of the exam, Marco's comprehension is limited. Piaget's theory seems abstract and "distant."
>
> Several days later Marco is at his community service placement with Head Start, working with pre-school children. While he interacts with the children, he begins thinking about Piaget's theory. That night he goes home and re-reads his notes on Piaget. They take on new meaning within the context of his experiences at Head Start. He starts re-constructing Piaget's theory for himself based upon his first-hand experience. Marco's individual construction of

this knowledge allows him to engage in dialogue on Piaget, explaining the theory *in his own words* and not merely repeating information.

In this case study, the professor originally conveyed knowledge to Marco in a manner that portrayed Piaget's theory as objective reality. Marco's community service activity with Head Start provided him with the opportunity to subjectively learn the theory, and construct his own knowledge. Personal constructivism allowed Marco to gain a deeper understanding of Piaget's theory, and move beyond knowledge repetition. In an ideal situation this connection would not be accidental. The professor would be aware of the volunteer activities of his or her students and would actively direct the theory based reflection in class or through a journal or other homework assignment.

Student affairs professionals involved would enhance students' learning by helping participants actively connect their course-based learning to their community service. While student affairs professionals might not understand the content and curriculum of all disciplines, understanding the processes which enhance students' cognitive development can put us in a better position to encourage students to subjectively construct their own knowledge. As student affairs professionals, we often view academic coursework as outside our domain. Conceptualizing learning as a seamless process compels student affairs professionals to assume responsibility for helping students integrate their service and learning and takes us beyond merely time management and study skills facilitation.

For example, the volunteer director who placed Marco in the Head Start agency might ask him about his courses, and then encourage him to think about service experience connections to his coursework. Since the basic tenet of social-constructivism is that knowledge is subjectively known and learned, the volunteer director need not have in-depth understanding of the students' course content. Instead, we can guide students in their personal process of linking learning to service, provide opportunities for reflection, and encourage students to discuss connections with classes or instructors.

Because service is not inherently linked to any specific academic discipline, we can assist students from a broad range of backgrounds in linking theory to practice. For example, another student volunteer at Head Start may be taking a sociology course. Through our discussions with the student, we might encourage the service participant to reflect on cultural capital and social reproduction theory that she has been studying in her courses.

Service-learning activities linked to the curriculum facilitate the discovery notion of learning. Students are provided with ample opportunities to re-construct the knowledge that has been conveyed in the classroom, and to discover and learn new constructs. Service-learning provides educators with the opportunity to engage students in discourse, and then facilitate the knowledge-construction process by providing students with activities related to the discourse. Social-constructivism and service-learning both place primacy on reflection on the physical activities in order to enhance knowledge (Driver et al, 1994; Kendall and Associates, 1990; Stanton, 1990). As student affairs professionals we are in a unique position to encourage student reflection on service, a critical component of service-learning that is often neglected in academic courses where service is considered an "add-on" to the curriculum.

Kolb's Learning Cycle

As described in Chapter 2, Kolb's (1984) learning cycle consists of a four-step process: (1) concrete experience involves direct, immediate experience, and a stimulation of the learners' feelings, (2) reflective observation involves intently observing experiences and reflecting on their meaning, (3) abstract conceptualization involves thinking and creating generalizations and concepts that organize experience, action and observations, and (4) active experimentation involves using generalizations or theories from the previous step to guide further action. The learner experiments by doing and testing what he or she has learned in new situations, resulting in further concrete experiences at more complex levels (Russell and Rothschadl, 1991). Kolb portrays this learning as a constantly revisited four-step cycle, and suggests an upward spiral movement of learning resulting from recycling through the model and building on past experiences (Stewart, 1990).

Service-learning programs are based upon some of the same central tenets as Kolb's experiential learning model. According to Kolb, learning integrally involves not only experience, but reflection, experimentation, and abstraction (Stewart, 1990). Service-learning programs are distinguished from community service programs on the same principle: learning involves more than experience alone (Kendall and Associates, 1990). Reflection and meaningful action that involves abstraction are considered critical components of service-learning (Kendall and Associates, 1990).

Kolb's experiential model provides a framework for understanding the learning process that occurs within service-learning programs. Students engage in community service activities (concrete experience), and reflect on their service experiences through journal writing or seminars (reflective observation). The reflection stimulates the student to organize observations, and create concepts to better understand the world and their service experiences (abstract conceptualization). This new understanding provides further confidence to experiment and act out theories (active experimentation), thereby enhancing learning and leading the student to revisit the cycle beginning with a new concrete experience (Stewart, 1990). Consider the following case study:

Tawanna Brown, a college senior majoring in social work, had been working at a local soup kitchen for a little over a year. Tawanna had been going faithfully to the soup kitchen once a week, enjoying her experience because it "made her feel good" and gave her a "helper's high." She had never thought about the volunteer work outside of the several hours each week she spent cutting vegetables and serving food.

This semester Tawanna enrolled in a service-learning social work course on poverty that requires a service component. Tawanna decided to continue her work at the soup kitchen since she enjoyed the experience. She uses that same experience as the basis for her journal writing, and other course requirements related to the service experience. As Tawanna writes in the journal about her experiences at the soup kitchen, she finds herself reflecting on issues of poverty and hunger. For the first time she thoughtfully and critically reflects on her experience and begins to make sense of it in the larger context of social issues in this country. Tawanna begins to apply theories from her social work course to her experience at the soup kitchen, and creates her own ideas on lessening the effects of poverty on low-income families.

Toward the end of the semester Tawanna organizes a coalition of campus and community groups to begin working on these ideas. She develops the confidence to bring one of her ideas to the coalition: providing apprenticeships within the agency (such as cooking classes, management opportunities coordinating the volunteers and advertising/public relations) for unemployed, low-income persons in the neighborhood. The apprenticeships are designed to empower low-income persons in the running of the agency, and to provide experience and skills that will assist in obtaining employment. The plan is well-received and implementation begins.

In accordance with Kolb's experiential model and service-learning models, Tawanna's learning was limited when she was involved in the service experience alone. Beyond cutting vegetables, and the "helper's high", there was little learning occurring during Tawanna's service experience at the soup kitchen. Once Tawanna's coursework prompts her to begin journal writing, she moves beyond the concrete experience to reflective observation. Tawanna's reflection, in conjunction with her coursework, leads her to abstract conceptualization about poverty and hunger in society. Eventually this leads Tawanna to active experimentation when she finds the confidence to experiment actively through the formation of a coalition that will work to implement her ideas. As her ideas regarding lessening the effects of poverty are implemented, she will revisit the four steps of the cycle, beginning again with new sets of concrete experiences. In this case, Tawanna's class was designed purposefully to create a link between the abstract conceptualization and reflective observation typically characteristic of classrooms, and the active experimentation and concrete experience at her service site.

Although Kolb's experiential learning model suggests that the four learning modes are sequential and that progression through all phases is important, individuals often develop preferences for one or two learning modes (Gish, 1979; Russell and Rothschadl, 1991). Kolb (1984) identified learners' strengths by four classifications: divergers, assimilators, accommodators, and convergers.

Service-learning can also enhance students' academic learning by providing opportunities to exercise both preferred and neglected modes (Gish, 1979). Formal classroom learning typically focuses on only one or two approaches, depending on the discipline (Gish, 1979). Service-learning offers opportunities to experiment with other modes, and strengthen neglected modes such as active experimentation and concrete experience.

The outcomes of utilizing service-learning to address all four modes of learning include broadening the learning capacity of students, and facilitating students' incorporation of additional learning approaches in their academic study (Gish, 1979). Since the most effective learning occurs when all four learning modes are utilized, service-learning's ability to address all modes would result in students more fully internalizing and retaining the skills and knowledge learned (Gish, 1979).

Self-efficacy

Chapter 2 describes how self-efficacy beliefs influence cognitive processes in a variety of forms, including personal goal setting, perceived ability and skill utilization, and the learning process (Bandura, 1993). Bandura (1993) notes that a distinct difference exists between possessing knowledge and skills and being able and willing to use them well. Variances in self-efficacy thinking can result in persons with the same knowledge and skills performing in radically different ways. Self-efficacy beliefs also influence the learning process. Persons who do not believe in their capabilities demonstrate a decreased capacity to learn, and individuals with high levels of self-efficacy have an increased ability to engage in complex learning (Bandura, 1993). In addition, beliefs of occupational efficacy are viewed as predominantly the product of socio-educational experiences (Bandura, 1994). Service-learning programs that provide environments where students can experiment with behaviors and learn new skills offer an opportunity for enhancing students' beliefs of self-efficacy. Consider the following case study:

Keung Hee Lin is a sophomore, interested in pursuing a degree in advertising. She is enrolled in an advertising course where she is currently at the top of the class. However, Keung Hee is not confident in her skills or abilities despite her good grades and performance to date. Several times when the professor requested her assistance with an assignment, she declined. She rarely speaks in class or volunteers her ideas. In a recent course-related workshop Keung Hee felt she was "in over her head". Keung Hee has difficulty finishing her assignment, even though she was more skilled and knowledgeable than most of the other students present. Subsequently, she contemplated not pursuing a degree or career in advertising because of self-doubts.

As an assignment for the course, Keung Hee is required to work with a volunteer student organization on an advertising campaign. Keung Hee works with a group called "Students Organized Against Poverty" on an ad campaign for their upcoming food drive. Keung Hee is confident working on this assignment since the ad campaign is small scale, working in a familiar environment with familiar mediums, and includes work with peers. Keung Hee's confidence and belief in her competencies in this particular situation allow her to perform extraordinarily. She uses her skills to develop a strong advertising campaign. The following summer, because of Keung Hee's enhanced sense of self-efficacy, she volunteers to develop a statewide advertising campaign for HIV+/AIDS education.

In the beginning of the case study, Keung Hee's low sense of self-efficacy regarding advertising results in her shying away from certain tasks, such as assisting the professor on an assignment. However, the service-learning experience provides Keung Hee with an opportunity to experiment with her abilities, and learn new skills. In the process, Keung Hee's sense of self-efficacy is enhanced, and she is able to utilize her potential and skills to successfully produce an advertising campaign. In turn, this personal accomplishment further increases her sense of efficacy, resulting in her confidence to set more challenging goals: developing a state-wide advertising campaign for HIV+/AIDS education.

Service-learning placements need to be tailored to students' needs and level of self-efficacy in order to be effective. A community service placement that is perceived as too far beyond the student's capabilities will be too threatening, and will decrease rather than increase their sense of self-efficacy.

With respect to this issue, student affairs professionals are in an excellent position to collaborate with faculty on service-learning initiatives. Often "service-learning" courses simply attach a service component to the curriculum as an option or requirement, with little attention to tailoring the student's service placement. Student affairs professionals are familiar with student development theories and self-esteem concepts, and volunteer directors are knowledgeable regarding community needs and responsibilities of volunteer positions in specific agencies. Working with faculty expectations regarding the service experience, student affairs professionals are in a unique position to tailor a service placement to student needs and self-efficacy. In addition, during the tenure of the placement, student affairs professionals can assist in the development of students' self-efficacy, which in turn can enhance learning.

Fortunately, in the case study the initial course assignment for Keung Hee was not overly threatening. Developing a small scale advertising campaign for a group of peers in a familiar environment provided a sense of security for Keung Hee. If the project had been perceived as a personal threat, Keung Hee's sense of efficacy might have been further damaged and she may have stopped pursuing her degree in advertising.

As evidenced by the case study, service-learning programs offer excellent opportunities for educators to provide avenues for students to increase their sense of self-efficacy. At the same time they require a delicate sense of balance between individual capabilities and the demands of the placement position. Armed with such experience, a firm sense of efficacy contributes to the type of social reality persons construct for themselves, and their subsequent learning, skill utilization, performance, and personal goal setting (Bandura, 1993; Bandura, 1994). As students engaged in service-learning programs grow more confident in their abilities, and develop a strong sense of self-efficacy, personal accomplishment and learning is significantly enhanced.

Freire's Conscientization

Freire's (1970) theory focuses on the social dimensions of learning. As described in Chapter 2, Freire's conscientization describes the process by which one moves from one level of consciousness to another, achieving a deepening awareness of one's socio-cultural reality (Elias, 1974; Freire, 1985). Learning as an active process that begins with the learner's ideas, words, and life situation. As described earlier, Freire's (1970) process of conscientization consists of four levels:

1. Intransitive consciousness, characterized by a preoccupation with meeting the most elementary needs, and no comprehension of one's sociocultural situation;

2. Semi-intransitivity, characterized by "cultures of silence," an external locus of control and self-depreciation;

3. Semi-transitive consciousness, characterized by the beginning of serious questioning of one's socio-cultural situation, and a sense that one has some control over their life; and

4. Critical consciousness, marked by depth in the interpretation of problems, self-confidence in discussion, receptiveness, responsibility, and scrutiny of thought (Elias, 1974).

Freire's (1970) novel view of education is as a process of critically reflecting on sociocultural and life situations. Journal writing, seminars, focus groups, and other methods of reflection used in service-learning programs foster this type of critical thinking. Although the theory does not focus on formal schooling (Bowers, 1987; Freire, 1970; Freire, 1985; Giroux, 1988), Freire's views are relevant to service-learning in higher education. Service-learning can provide a mechanism for moving learners from one level of consciousness to another. Students engaged in activities in the community can develop an increased awareness of sociocultural situations. Students involved in community agencies that foster activism can also develop a stronger locus of control, and increased sense of empowerment in their lives. And students engaged in the critical reflection component of service-learning will evidence a depth of interpretation of problems characteristic of the critical consciousness level. Consider the following case study:

> David Jimenez is a first-generation college student from the inner city of New York. David is actually the first person from his neighborhood, a predominantly Puerto Rican and African-American community, to attend college. David feels "lucky" to be attending college, but has not given much thought to the fact that he is the first person in his family, or neighborhood, to attend an institution of higher education. Most of David's time, energy and thought are given to meeting his most basic needs and "getting by": working many hours to pay tuition and housing costs, studying, and making weekend trips back "home" to help his mother care for his younger sisters.
>
> A seminar David enrolled in this semester, "History of Race and Ethnicity in the United States," requires a community service placement at a human service agency. As David works with underprivileged youth at a local boys club, and studies the "theory of the underclass" in his coursework, he becomes aware of the history of oppression affecting persons of color. He critically examines his first-generation college student status in a new light. Upon returning to his neighborhood one weekend, David becomes more conscious of the sociocultural reality of his family and friends, and his own personal situation.
>
> His coursework, and subsequent historical understanding of oppression, allow David to begin seriously questioning life's situations; and focus groups associated with the service-learning course foster David's critical reflection. As the semester progresses, David's critical reflection and depth of understanding of oppression result in a strong self-confidence when discussing issues in his focus groups and class. David begins to feel a sense of responsibility to work against oppression, and becomes actively involved in a local activist organization that struggles against forms of domination.

In this case study, David is initially at the "intransitive consciousness" level. He is unaware of the sociocultural situation, and is preoccupied with meeting his basic survival needs. David's service-learning experience with disadvantaged youth at a boys club allows him to become increasingly aware of forms of oppression. His coursework, focus group, and service-learning reflective component cause David to begin to seriously question forms of domination, and enter the "semi-transitive consciousness level." Finally, David moves beyond his previous complacency to a level of "critical consciousness." David becomes an activist, confident in his understanding of oppression and ability to articulate his ideas. Subsequently, he works as a "teacher" or co-investigator to make other learners aware of their life situations, and encourages others to challenge forms of domination.

The following summer David helps organize youth in his neighborhood, and as he engages them in dialogue regarding issues of oppression, the youth increasingly become aware of their sociocultural reality. The youth begin to believe that they have some control over their lives, and slowly become empowered to work with David on new initiatives that can help create change for their community.

In this case study, David's depth of understanding and interpretation of course concepts may have been hampered without his service placement. Ideas and theories may have remained too abstract and "distant" in a traditional course. According to Freire's theory, conscientization must begin with the learners' ideas, words and life situation. Service-learning was integral to David's learning in this case study since his service placement allowed his learning, and process of conscientization, to begin with ideas, words and a "life situation" familiar to him. Thus, he could more easily move beyond abstract concepts and academic rhetoric. The service placement allows David to grapple intellectually with genuine issues that concerned his community. However, in the traditional classroom context students often lack any way to act on their beliefs (Seigel and Rockwood, 1993). In this case study, David's service-learning experience provides a unique opportunity for David to act on his beliefs and learning.

Given the activism and educational components inherent in most human service agencies, Freire's view of learning is easily applicable to service-learning. Both the servers and those served benefit from the process of conscientization that increases awareness of sociocultural situations and oppression. The servers learn that they themselves, as well as the help they provide, are part of the system that oppresses. Freire's theory of learning is often criticized for its strong emphasis on the political nature of education, and view that education is always political (Elias, 1974). However, service-learning programs' connection to human service agencies and social issues (domestic violence, hunger and homelessness, illiteracy, etc.) is inherently political, creating a natural connection between Freire's theory and service-learning.

Conscientization's emphasis on critical reflection (Bowers, 1987), and service-learning's emphasis on critical reflection (Kendall and Associates, 1990), also create a natural connection between Freire's theory and service-learning. In addition, service-learning programs address other components of Freire's learning: teacher and student engage in dialogue and are co-investigators in the learning process, and teacher and learner are jointly responsible for learning. In addition, service-learning placements can provide an approach that allows students to begin the learning process within their own reality, values, and life-situation.

Freire (1970) emphasizes the need to provide those served with the right to speak and be heard in order to emancipate them from the "culture of silence". This emphasis is also integral to service-learning in order to avoid "patronizing charity" that fosters a power imbalance where the "haves" provide for the "have-nots". The Campus Opportunity Outreach League (COOL) states that "community voice" is a critical component of service-learning programs (Kendall and Associates, 1990).

Discussion

Student affairs professionals can benefit from understanding the connections between theory and practice. Learning theories applied to student affairs venues, such as service-learning, allows us to frame learning as a joint responsibility of both academic and student affairs. We need to be able to articulate our common goals in enhancing students' cognitive and personal development, and understand not just "what" students learn, but "how" learning occurs within such venues. Both academic and student affairs will benefit from the collaborative approach to learning. And students will also benefit as in-class learning and cognitive development are enhanced, and the learning associated with community service is maximized.

As student affairs professionals and faculty acknowledge their common goals through initiatives that strengthen the integration of service and learning, service-learning can be re-framed as a fundamental part of students' core learning activities. As higher education increasingly focuses on the cognitive learning outcomes associated with service-learning, there may arise a tendency for higher education institutions to reallocate responsibilities for service to academic departments. However, this restructuring may result in the loss of an opportunity to engage in a holistic systems approach that closely links academic and student affairs professionals.

In addition to working with faculty collaboratively on service-learning courses, we also need find ways to integrate intentional learning goals into non-academic based community service. Despite the growth of the service-learning movement, volunteerism and community service are still the predominant mode of involvement for college students (American College Personnel Association, 1994; O'Brien, 1993). Since the majority of volunteerism still occurs outside the formal academic curriculum, valuable student learning opportunities will be lost if we limit service-learning to the domain of academic courses. Within the non-academic based community service settings, we can help students connect service-learning activities to their studies through strategies such as reflection groups, one-on-one discussions, and journals.

Conclusion

This chapter applies four learning theories to service-learning programs: social-constructivism, Kolb's learning cycle, self-efficacy, and Freire's conscientization. The application of these learning theories provides insights into the cognitive development that occurs through the intentional combination of service and learning. Educators need to continue to explore the relationship between cognitive development and service-learning, and to ensure that curricular and co-curricular programs both contain the critical elements needed to effectively combine service and learning. We are losing valuable learning opportunities when co-curricular community service programs neglect students cognitive learning and reflection. Similarly, we are losing learning opportunities when academic based service-learning takes the form of two separate and distinct activities co-existing within the framework of a single course: learning activities inside the classroom, service activities outside the classroom.

Further quantitative and qualitative research is needed to increase our understanding of the impact of service-learning programs on student learning. In addition, there is a need to explore the application of additional learning theories to service-learning programs. Learning theories from fields such as psychology, sociology, and philosophy will broaden our perspectives and increase our abilities to take advantage of rich opportunities for combining service and learning.

Explicitly linking service to the academic curriculum is more than an effort to ensuring "survival" of the latest community service movement of the 1990s. Service-learning provides a means to capitalize on students' learning process by directly applying learning theories to practice. As student affairs professionals, we will benefit from our knowledge and understanding of students' learning process and how service contributes to students' cognitive and personal development. We will be better able to collaboratively work with faculty to integrate what occurs inside the formal classroom and outside the classroom during the students' service activities and together facilitate the learning process.

References

American College Personnel Association (1994). *The student learning imperative: Implications for student affairs.* Alexandria, VA: American College Personnel Association.

Bandura, A. (1993). Perceived self-efficacy in cognitive development and functioning. *Educational Psychologist, 28*(2), 117–148.

Bandura, A. (1994). *Self-efficacy concerns of adulthood.* (personal manuscript).

Barber, B., and Battistoni, R. (1993). A season of service: Introducing service-learning into the liberal arts curriculum. *PS: Political Science and Politics, 26,* 235–240, 262.

Batchelder, T. H., and Root, S. (1994). Effects of an undergraduate program to integrate academic learning and service: cognitive, prosocial cognitive, and identity outcomes. *Journal of Adolescence, 17,* 341–355.

Bowers, C. A. (1987). Paulo Freire. *Elements of a post-liberal theory of education.* N.Y.: Teachers College Press.

Bringle, R. G., and Hatcher, J. A. (1996). Implementing service learning in higher education. *Journal of Higher Education, 67*(2), 221–239.

Cobb, P. (1994). Where is the mind? Constructivist and sociocultural perspectives on mathematical development. *Educational Researcher, 23*(7), 13–20.

Conrad, C., and Hedin, D. (1982). The impact of experiential education on adolescent development. *Child and Youth Services, 4*, 57–76.

Delve, C. I., Mintz, S. D. and Stewart, G. M. (1990). *Community service as values education, New Directions for Student Services*, No. 50. San Francisco: Jossey-Bass.

Dewey, J. (1916). *Democracy and education: An introduction to the philosophy of education.* New York: Macmillan.

Driver, R., Asoko, H., Leach, J., Mortimer, E., and Scott, P. (1994). Constructing scientific knowledge in the classroom. *Educational Researcher, 23*(7), 5–12.

Elias, J. L. (1974). Social learning and Paulo Freire. *The Journal of Educational Thought, 8*, 5–14.

Freire, P. (1970). *Pedagogy of the oppressed.* New York: Herder and Herder.

Freire, P. (1985). *An invitation to conscientization and deschooling. The politics of education.* South Hadley: Bergin and Garvey.

Giles, Jr., D. E., and Eyler, J. (1994). The impact of a college community service laboratory on students' personal, social and cognitive outcomes. *Journal of Adolescence, 17,* 327–339.

Giroux, H. A. (1988). Culture, power and transformation in the work of Paulo Freire: Toward a politics of education. *Teachers as intellectuals.* MA: Bergin and Garvey.

Gish, G. L. (1979). The learning cycle. *Synergist: National Center for Service-Learning, 8*(3), 2–6.

Hamilton, S. F., and Fenzel, L. M. (1988). The impact of volunteer experiences on adolescent social development: Evidence of program effects. *Journal of Adolescent Research, 3*, 65–80.

Jacoby, B. and Associates (1996). *Service-learning in higher education: Concepts and practices.* San Francisco: Jossey-Bass.

Kendall, J. C. and Associates (Eds.). (1990). *Combining service and learning: A resource book for community and public service* (Vols. 1–2). Raleigh, NC: National Society for Experiential Education.

Kolb, D. A. (1984). *Experiential learning: Experience as the source of learning and development.* New York: Prentice-Hall.

Marcus, G. B., Howard, J. P. F., and King, D. C. (1993). Integrating community service and classroom instruction enhances learning: Results from an experiment. *Educational Evaluation and Policy Analysis, 15*(4), 410–419.

O'Brien, E. M. (1993). *Outside the classroom: Students as employees, volunteers, and interns* (Research Briefs, Vol. 4, No. 1). Washington, DC: American Council on Education, Division of Policy Analysis and Research.

Radest, H. B. (1993). *Community Service: Encounter with Strangers*. Westport, CT: Praeger Publishers.

Rhoads, R. A. (1997). *Community service and higher learning: Explorations of the caring self*. Albany: SUNY Press.

Russell, R. and Rothschadl, A. (1991). Learning Styles: Another view of the college classroom? *Schole: A journal of recreation education and leisure studies, 6*, 34–45.

Schine, J. (1995). Community Service: When theory and practice meet. *Educational Researcher, 24*(2), 33–35.

Seigel, S., and Rockwood, V. (1993). Democratic education, student empowerment, and community service: Theory and practice. *Equity and Excellence in Education, 26*(2), 65–70.

Stanton, T. (1990). *Integrating public service with academic study: The faculty role*. Providence, RI: Campus Compact.

Stewart, G. M. (1990). Learning styles as a filter for developing service-learning interventions. In C. I. Delve, S. D. Mintz and G. M. Stewart (Eds.), *Community service as values education, New Directions for Student Services*, No. 50 (pp. 31–42). San Francisco: Jossey-Bass.

Tyler, R. (1949). *Basic principles of curriculum and instruction*. Chicago: University of Chicago Press.

Zlotkowski, E. (1996). A new voice at the table? Linking service-learning and the academy. *Change, 28*(1), 20–27.

7

Assessing
Student Learning

M. Lee Upcraft

The discussion in previous chapters of the importance of student learning as a guiding framework for student affairs assumes that what we do has some influence on this outcome. More specifically, "Of those persons who use our services, programs, and facilities, is there any effect on their learning, development, academic success, or other intended outcomes, particularly when compared to non-users? Can institutional interventions (for example, programs, services, and policies) be isolated from other variables that may influence outcomes, such as background and entering characteristics, described by Watson and Stage in Chapter 1, and other collegiate and non-collegiate experiences?" (Upcraft and Schuh, 1996).

All of this was not lost on the creators of the Student Learning Imperative (SLI). The document itself poses the question, ". . . if learning is the primary measure of institutional productivity by which

This article is based in part on "Assessment Strategies for the Student Learning Imperative" By Ernest T. Pascarella and M. Lee Upcraft (in press), in E. Whitt (ed.), *The Student Learning Imperative*. Washington, D.C.: National Association of Student Personnel Administrators.

the quality of undergraduate education is determined, what and how much students learn must be the criterion by which the value of student affairs is judged" (ACPA, 1994, p. 2). In addition, Chapters 1 and 2 reiterate the specific ways in which we may approach an understanding of our students in order to improve their educational outcomes. This is no small challenge, and assumes we have the wherewithal to demonstrate, in systematic ways, how what we do affects student learning. In other words, how well we can assess what we do.

This chapter reviews why assessment is essential to higher education and student affairs today, provides some definitions to frame the discussion, suggests several student learning outcomes based on the SLI, and offers two specific examples of how student learning might be assessed.

Why Assessment in Higher Education and Student Affairs

When the assessment movement first gained momentum in the 1970s, there were many who thought it was yet another higher education "fad" that would quickly fade from the scene. They were wrong. In the 1980s several national reports within higher education called for a greater emphasis on assessment in higher education. In the 1990s, tough questions are being asked. As summarized by Terenzini (1989), these questions include: What should one get from a college education? What should one get from a college education at this institution? And the most important question of all: How do we know? Similar questions are asked in Watson's (1996) conceptual framework presented in chapter one. Who are our students? What were their home and school environments like? How will these "input" factors affect the college experiences "process" and their educational outcomes? By asking these questions in our planning, we enhance our ability to evaluate and assess their "true" learning.

Many factors have contributed to the current pressure to assess. First, too many examples exist of people with college degrees who appear to be uneducated, even in the most basic sense of that term: graduates unable to read, write, compute, or do anything else indicative of an educated person. Second, the public is increasingly dissatisfied because of the rising cost of higher education, and the question is being asked, "Is it worth it?" Third, there is increasing dissatisfaction with the quality of instruction at many institutions, including large classes, fewer faculty who actually teach, poor academic advising, failure to do anything about poor teaching, and so forth. Fourth, and no less important, are the issues of access and equity in higher education, including the alarming discrepancy between the success rates of traditionally underrepresented groups and those of the majority. And finally, assessment is now a required part of the accreditation of higher education institutions (Upcraft and Schuh, 1996).

To these questions of accountability, cost, quality, access, equity, and accreditation is added the question: in a era of declining resources, are student services really necessary? This fundamental question about the purpose of student affairs in higher education was outlined in Chapter 1. If the role of student affairs is to contribute to student learning, then three more questions follow: How do student programs and services contribute to student learning? How do we know? And what tools are available to us to assess student learning?

Unfortunately, there is a natural tendency for institutions to reallocate resources to their academic priorities, narrowly interpreted as support for the faculty, the classroom the formal curriculum, and those support services that are clearly academically related, such as learning support centers and academic advising. However, this narrow focus ignores substantial evidence (summarized by Pascarella and Terenzini, 1991, and Kuh et al, 1994), that the out-of-class experiences of students are important factors in learning, development, academic achievement, and retention, and that student services and programs contribute to those outcomes (Upcraft and Schuh, 1996). In short, student affairs must respond not only to the global pressures identified above, but also to enormous internal pressure to justify allocation of resources to programs and services that appear to the "nonacademic" and therefore "less essential" to the educational enterprise.

Upcraft and Schuh (1996) assert many other reasons, besides justifying our existence or preventing our demise, that student affairs should have a commitment to assessment. Even if the basic question of the value of student affairs to the institution has been answered affirmatively, assessment has many other uses. It provides important information to deal with issues such as quality improvement, affordability, and cost effectiveness. It is also important in strategic planning, policy development and decision making, and dealing with various political constituencies inside and outside the institution.

For all these reasons, assessment is no longer in the "nice if you can afford it" category. It now moves to the "you had better have it if you want to survive and improve" category. The *Student Learning Imperative* (SLI) is an important first step in this transformation because a provides a restatement of the rationale for our profession that is more inclusive ("student learning"), and implies a set of measurable objectives that provide the basis for an assessment agenda that can address the issues identified above.

Some Basic Definitions

One of the causes of confusion about assessment is terminology. While there are many definitions of assessment, for the purposes of this chapter, we will use Upcraft and Schuh's (1996) definition: "*Assessment* is any effort to gather, analyze, and interpret evidence that describes institutional, departmental, divisional, or agency effectiveness" (p. 18). Upcraft and Schuh (1996) also argue that assessment must be contrasted with but also linked to the concept of *evaluation*, defined as "any effort to use assessment evidence to improve institutional, departmental, divisional, or agency effectiveness" (p. 19). Put another way, while assessment describes effectiveness, evaluation is the application of assessment evidence to improve effectiveness, however that might be defined by an institution, department, division, or agency.

Another term that muddies the definitional waters is *research*. When comparing research and assessment, Erwin (1991) argues that although they share many processes in common, they differ in at least two respects. First, assessment guides good practice, while research guides theory and conceptual foundations. Second, assessment typically has implications for a single institution, while research typically has broader implications for student affairs and higher education.

To summarize, given these definitions, this chapter is about primarily assessment and evaluation, although there may be some implications for research.

Assessing Student Learning Outcomes

We now return to the question posed at the beginning of this chapter. What impact, if any, does student affairs have on student learning, and how will we know? We can base our services, programs, and facilities on the set of assumptions for student affairs work provided by the SLI, but if these have no impact on selected student outcomes, then the SLI becomes yet another interesting but irrelevant statement of the purposes and goals of student affairs. So the focus of the rest of this chapter is to provide a framework for assessing student learning outcomes based on the SLI.

Watson's (1996) model presented in Chapter 1 is an excellent example of a contemporary refinement of Astin's (1991) input-environment-outcome (I-E-O) framework and provides us with an excellent design for assessing outcomes. As described in chapter one, educational outcomes are the result of the wide variety of personal, background, and educational characteristics that students bring to college (inputs), and the wide variety of student experiences once they enroll (process). Only when both inputs and experiences are taken into account may one explain a particular outcome or output.

Terenzini and Upcraft (1996) argue that the first step in the outcomes assessment process is to determine outcomes. Once outcomes have been determined, then one may select which inputs and experiences may be relevant to those outcomes, based on previous research and other factors relevant to the purposes of the study.

In recognition of this basic principle, in January of 1995, John Dalton, then president of the National Association of Student Personnel Administrators, assembled a group of educators and practitioners to develop student learning outcomes based on the *SLI*. After several days of deliberation, and much spirited discussion, this group identified six outcomes, imbedded in current literature and research, upon which student learning might be assessed. They include:

1. Complex cognitive skills: Reflective thought, critical thinking, quantitative reasoning, and intellectual flexibility.

2. Knowledge acquisition: Subject matter mastery and knowledge application.

3. Intrapersonal development: Autonomy, values, identity, aesthetics, self esteem, and maturity.

4. Interpersonal development: Understanding and appreciating human differences, ability to relate to others, and establishing intimate relationships.

5. Practical competence: Career preparation, managing one's personal affairs, and economic self-sufficiency.

6. Civic responsibility: Responsibilities as a citizen in a democratic society and commitment to democratic ideals.

And two more additions:

7. Academic achievement: Ability to earn satisfactory grades in courses.

8. Persistence: Ability to pursue a degree to graduation.

These eight then can form the basis for nearly any plan for college student assessment. Pascarella and Terenzini's (1991) review of nearly 3,000 studies of college students found that students' educational achievements closely parallel other kinds of learning and personal development gains. Now our question is, how does one design a study that investigates the relationship of the unique contributions of an institution's programmatic and policy actions to these outcomes?

Assessment Design Options

Once a model of outcomes assessment has been decided (in this instance, Astin's IEO model described above was used, although the process model suggested by Watson and Stage in Chapter 1 would also be quite useful), and viable outcomes have been selected, one must decide how to go about assessing a particular problem or issue. There are basically three choices: quantitative methods, qualitative methods, or combinations of both.

As summarized by Upcraft and Schuh (1996), in general, quantitative methodology is the assignment of numbers to objects, events, or observations according to some rule (Rossman and El-Khawas, 1987). Patton (1990) adds that quantitative methods require the use of standard measures so that the varying perspectives and experiences of people can be fit into a limited number of predetermined response categories to which numbers are assigned. Thus it is possible to measure the reactions of a great many people by way of a limited set of questions, facilitating comparisons and statistical aggregation and analysis of data. According to Shulman (1988), in quantitative research, samples are drawn from populations in ways that ensure that those chosen are representative of the population, according to some criteria. If the sample is, in fact, representative, then one can confidently generalize the findings from the sample to the whole population.

On the other hand, qualitative approaches include detailed descriptions of situations, events, people, interactions, and observed behaviors; use of direct quotations from people about their experiences, observations, attitudes, beliefs, and thoughts; and analysis of excerpts or entire passages from documents, correspondence, records, and histories (Patton, 1990; Stage, 1992; Wolcott, 1990).

Of course, these methodologies can be combined. For example, one could administer the *College Student Experiences Questionnaire* (CSEQ) (Pace, 1988) to assess how students describe their collegiate experiences, and also conduct focus groups or individual interviews covering the same topics. Together, these approaches would yield a more complete assessment of student perceptions. (See Russell and Stage (1992) and Shulman (1988) for a discussion of the use of combined methodologies).

Deciding which approaches to use is much more complicated and well beyond space limitations of this chapter; however, factors to be taken into account include the purpose of the study, the outcomes selected, resources available, convenience of data collection, the competence of those analyzing the data, and the audience to whom the results will be directed.

The latter point is especially important because in many academic environments a built-in bias exists against qualitative approaches. Thus using both approaches in the same study is recommended. If qualitative methods are used exclusively, then as long as such skepticism exists, the report of findings must educate readers about the validity of these methodologies.

Assessing Student Learning: A Quantitative Approach

Suppose skeptics are questioning the allocation of resources to student activities. Let's further assume that the Office of Student Activities, as a progressive unit, has identified civic responsibility (one of the student learning outcomes suggested above) as an important outcome of their efforts. Let's further assume this outcome has been operationalized through a two-credit leadership development course, offered to students leaders, designed and taught by student affairs staff. And finally, let's assume that the continuing funding of this program is being challenged by the institution's budget committee on the assumption that there is no evidence that the program develops leadership skills.

According to Terenzini and Upcraft (1996), a very basic yet credible quantitative design should proceed according to the following steps:

1. Define the Problem

In this instance, the problem is the threat of discontinued funding for a program believed to have value to students.

2. Determine the Purposes of the Study

The purpose is to determine to what extent, if any, students in a class on leadership development show improvement in their leadership skills, compared to those who did not take the course.

3. Define the Appropriate Assessment Approach

In this instance, Watson's, input-process-output model is selected, because there is an attempt to show the impact of a particular environmental intervention, or process, on a selected outcome, taking into account initial differences.

4. Determine the Outcomes

The outcome selected for this study is leadership skills.

5. Identify the Input or Control Variables

Watson and Stage, in chapter one suggest possible input variables that include previous educational experiences as well as home and community experiences in addition to more typical student characteristics. Most institutions have access to a dozen or so standard input variables. Other variables such as involvement in community projects or past experience with group conflict would have to be solicited through a questionnaire if the evaluator decided that they had direct relevance to the purpose of the study. In this case, the pretest on leadership skills could be used as a control for the effects of previous experience. Since evidence exists that leadership skills may be influenced by participant characteristics, the control variables selected for this study include race/ethnicity, gender, and class standing. A pre-course measure of leadership skills is also necessary.

6. Identify the Process or Environmental Variables

This is a very tricky area, since so many other experiences in the college environment might well influence the development of students' leadership skills. Again, the pretest on leadership skills could be used as a control for the effects of college experiences prior to that semester. While all current environmental variables would be impossible to gather, the investigator must select the ones that appear to be the most relevant and available. In this instance, the extent of past and present involvement in student leadership positions was identified as the most important environmental variable, along with place of residence, number of hours worked, and grade point average.

7. Select the Measurement Instruments

After a careful review of the instruments available that best reflected the goals and content of the leadership course, the *Leadership Practices Inventory (LPI)*, by Kouzes and Posner (1990) was selected. This instrument yields five leadership practices that are common to most leadership achievements, including *challenging the process, inspiring a shared vision, enabling others to act, modeling the way, and encouraging the heart.*

8. Determine the Population to be Studied and the Sample to be Drawn

For this study, the population was all undergraduate students. One sample (the experimental group) included all the students in the leadership course, and the other sample (control group) included a sample of undergraduates whose characteristics matched those in the control group by gender, age, and class standing.

9. Determine the Modes of Statistical Analyses

Because of the complexity of the assessment model, a multivariate analysis was chosen because this array of statistical tools can control for input variables, take into account process variables, and determine the unique outcomes, if any, of taking the leadership course.

10. Develop and Implement a Plan for Data Collection

Data were collected from course participants and the control group, including background characteristics and the LPI, at the beginning of the semester. At the end of the semester, the LPI was administered again to both groups, and data was collected on the environmental variables cited above.

11. Record the Data in Useable Form

Data were recorded in an electronic data base for analysis.

12. Conduct the Appropriate Analyses

The database was analyzed using the SPSS statistical package to run multiple regression analyses. In this instance, class participants showed statistically significant greater gains in leadership skills than the control group on all five leadership dimensions.

Assessing Student Learning:
A Qualitative Approach

Using the same scenario as the quantitative study described above, how might a qualitative study be designed to deal with the same issue. The steps required are in some ways similar to the quantitative approach, but differ in many significant ways.

1. Define the Problem

The problem remains the same: the threat of discontinued funding for a program believed to be have value for students.

2. Determine the Purposes of the Study

The purpose is somewhat different: to gain a more indepth insight into how and why students in a class on leadership development showed improvement in their leadership skills.

3. Determine the Appropriate Assessment Approach

Because the purpose is to gain insight into student perceptions, a qualitative approach was selected.

4. Select the Assessment Instrument

An individual interview protocol was selected, based on the model of leadership development that guided the course, asking students to reflect upon their experiences in the class, based on course content and class activities. Patton (1990) identifies six types of questions that might be considered: experience and behavior questions, opinion and values questions, feeling questions, knowledge questions, sensory questions, and background and demographic questions.

5. Determine the Population to be Studied, and the Sample to be Drawn

In this instance, it was decided to interview all of the students in the leadership class, so sampling was not an issue. However, in instances where sampling is necessary, Patton (1990) identifies fifteen different qualitative sampling methods, such as maximum variation sampling, typical case sampling, stratified purposeful sampling, snowball or chain sampling, criterion sampling, purposeful random sampling, and others. The best sampling procedure is the one that best fits the purpose of a particular study. It should be noted, however that while representativeness of the sample is important in qualitative studies, it may not be necessary, again depending upon the purpose of the study.

6. Determine How the Information Will Be Collected

Post-class interviews were conducted by professional staff who did not teach the course, asking students about their experiences in the class, based on the interview protocol described above.

7. Determine How the Information Will Be Codified

Typically, individual interviews yield an enormous amount of data that must be codified, organized, and sequenced in ways that make analyses possible. (For a more complete discussion on techniques to manage qualitative data, see Patton, 1990).

8. Determine How the Information Will Be Analyzed

This is the "what does it all mean" step. Unlike quantitative analyses, there are few agreed upon rules for qualitative data analysis, no formulas for determining significance, no ways of replicating the researcher's analytical thought processes, and no straightforward tests for reliability and validity. The challenge of analyzing qualitative data is to try to make sense out of data, identify significant patterns, and construct a framework for communicating the essence of what the data reveal (Patton, 1990). Upcraft and Schuh (1996) suggest that investigators to keep discussing, probing, and thinking until a consensus is reached on "what it all means." It is also entirely possible that more data will need to be collected from those interviewed in order to make the analysis complete (For brief introductions to qualitative data analysis methods see Stage, 1992 and for detailed discussions see Patton, 1990 or Lincoln and Guba, 1985).

Evaluation: The Final and Most Important Step in the Assessment Process

Earlier in this chapter, assessment was defined as any effort to gather, analyze, and interpret evidence that describes institutional, departmental, divisional, or agency effectiveness, while evaluation was defined as any effort to use assessment evidence to improve effectiveness. According to Upcraft and Schuh (1996), too often, even the best designed and most carefully reported studies end up gathering dust on someone's shelf because the institution failed to take advantage of the results, for whatever reasons: lack of resources, lack of courage to implement the recommendations, indecisiveness, or fear of political or public reaction. While no amount of planning will necessarily prevent a study's being ignored, some things can be done to enhance the likelihood that a study will be used to improve effectiveness.

The traditional approach for assessment studies is to present the findings, and leave the evaluation to the appropriate administrator. In my opinion, this is a serious mistake. An investigator must not only report findings, but outline the implications of the findings for policy and practice, and suggest a plan using the results.

Getting back to our two studies, two additional steps are involved in the evaluation process.

1. Evaluate the Analyses for Policy and Practice Implications

The report of these studies suggested that the findings had several implications for policy and practice:

- Recommended that the course continue to be offered, but expanded to include more students;

- Offered suggestions for how the course content might be revised and expanded;

- Suggested the course might be adapted to students in academic majors whose curricula intend to develop leadership skills;

- Suggested that other courses, modeled on this one, be proposed in areas such as alcohol abuse, orientation, and service learning.

The report was submitted to the Vice-president for Student Affairs, who met with the investigators to discuss the findings, so that she would have a clear understanding of the studies, and their implications for policy and practice.

2. Develop a Strategy for Using the Results

The report suggested that the Vice-president for Student Affairs send summaries of the studies to appropriate student affairs staff, and offer them an opportunity to comment upon the results, either in writing, or in a face to face meeting with the investigators.

The report also suggested that individually tailored summaries of the report be sent to the president, the chief academic officers, the chair of the budget committee, and the deans of the colleges, with a cover letter that specifically identified the implications of the studies for each person. In addition, the report suggested that the Vice-President make a presentation of the findings to the faculty senate.

Further, the report suggested that the Vice-President

1) Appoint a team of student affairs staff to revise and expand the course;

2) Approach the Engineering School with a proposal to collaborate on leadership in engineering program for engineering majors;

3) Include a summary of the report in her next budget presentation; and

4) Appoint a team to develop courses for credit for other topics, including alcohol education, orientation, and service learning.

Summary

Watson's (1996) model provides structure to an assessment of learning that takes place on a college campus. The strength of the SLI is that it provides us a framework within which we bridge the chasm between students' academic and personal development, help student make connections between their academic and out-of-class experiences, and provide a basis for a working relationship between student affairs and academic affairs. But as the creators of the SLI made very clear, the key is assessment, and our ability to demonstrate, in systematic ways, how our services, programs, and facilities influence student learning.

References

American College Personnel Association (1994). *Student learning imperative: Implications*

Astin, A. W. (1991). *Assessment for excellence*. New York: Macmillan.*for student affairs*. Alexandria, VA: American College Personnel Association.

Astin, A. W. (1993). *What matters in college: Four critical years revisited*. San Francisco: Jossey-Bass.

Kouzes, J. M. and Posner, B. Z. (1990). *The leadership practices inventory (LPI): A self assessment and analysis*. San Diego: Pfeiffer.

Kuh, G. D., Douglas, K. B., Lund, J. P., and Ramin-Gyurnek, J. (1994). *Student learning outside the classroom: Transcending artificial boundaries.* ASHE-ERIC Higher Education Report No. 8. Washington, DC: The George Washington University, School of Education and Human Development.

Lincoln, Y. S. and Guba, E. G., (1985). *Naturalistic inquiry.* Newbury Park, CA: Sage.

Pace, C. R. (1988). *CSEQ: Test manual and norms.* University of California, Los Angeles: Center for the study of evaluation.

Pascarella, E. T. and Terenzini, P. T. (1991). *How college affects students: Findings and insights from twenty years of research.* San Francisco: Jossey-Bass.

Patton, M. Q. (1990). *Qualitative evaluation and research methods.* (2nd ed.) Newbury Park, CA: Sage.

Rossman, J. E. and El-Khawas, E. (1987). *Thinking about assessment: Perspectives for presidents and chief academic officers.* Washington, DC: American Council on Education and the American Association for Higher Education.

Russell, R. V. and Stage, F. K. (1992). "Triangulation: Intersecting Assessment and Research Methods." In F. K. Stage (ed.), *Diverse methods for research and assessment of college students.* Alexandria, VA: American College Personnel Association.

Shulman, L. S. (1988). "Disciplines of inquiry in education: An overview." In R. Jaeger (ed.), *Complimentary methods for research in education.* Washington, DC: American Educational Research Association.

Stage, F. K. (1992). "The case for flexibility in research and assessment of college students." In F. K. Stage (ed.), *Diverse methods for research and assessment of college students.* Alexandria, VA: American College Personnel Association.

Terenzini, P. T. (1989). "Assessment with open eyes: Pitfalls in studying student outcomes." *Journal of Higher Education,* 60(6), 644–664.

Terenzini, P. T. and Upcraft, M. L. (1996). "Assessing program and service outcomes" from Upcraft, M. L. and Schuh, J. H. *Assessment in student affairs: A guide for practitioners.* San Francisco: Jossey-Bass.

Upcraft, M. Lee and Schuh, J. H. (1996). *Assessment in student affairs: A guide for practitioners.* San Francisco: Jossey-Bass.

Watson, L.W. (1996). A collaborative approach to student learning: A model for administrators in higher education. *Planning and Changing: An Educational Leeadership and Policy Journal.*

Wolcott, H. F. (1990). *Writing up qualitative Research.* Qualitative Research Methods, no. 20. Newbury Park, CA: Sage

8

Setting a New Context for Student Learning

Frances K. Stage
Lemuel W. Watson

Shirley Heath and Milbrey McLaughlin (1994) in a recent article "Learning for anything everyday" argued that academic foci on learning typically ignore learning that takes place in everyday life. Speaking to educators, they focus on the curriculum of youth organizations—Boy and Girl Scouts, grassroots athletic organizations, and apprenticeship experiences as they relate to learning. They propose that such experiences might provide the bases for 'authentic' experiences and evaluation being widely sought in all aspects of elementary and secondary education (Delandshere and Petrosky, 1994).

If the argument sounds familiar to those in student affairs—it should. Many of us have engaged in campus discussions about the value of learning in the student affairs context as well as possible links to classroom learning. Pat Hutchings (1992) refers us to many who, a decade ago, began to assess such learning; probably the most familiar are the folks at Alverno (Mentkowski and Doherty, 1984). The conceptual framework in Chapter 1 and the theories of learning in chapter two could help us to extend those discussions. And following Heath and McLaughlin's advice, we might make efforts to evaluate such learning experiences as evidence of the "authenticity" of college students' learning.

Consider the following examples. A service-learning program that links experience to classroom based theories of learning could be evaluated by comparing the related class outcomes for students who participated in the service activities with the outcomes for students who did not (controlling for initial abilities). For student leaders, leadership abilities might be evaluated and then compared to their abilities after linking their experiences with theories of group behavior and leadership.

Students who struggle with grades and are placed on academic probation might be encouraged to take a lighter course load, take a learning skills development course, and engage in a limited way in activities and experiences congruent with past successes. Looking more closely at who the student is provides cues for positive probationary tasks. A former high school swimmer might be given internship credits for managing the swimming team; a business major might be encouraged to work as an intern for 10 hours a week with a city program for start-up businesses; and a natural resource major might work with physical plant operations on campus. These students could gain reinforcement for expansion of their already strong skills, acquire knowledge and experiences that help develop self-efficacy, and build motivation to work toward academic goals. In addition, they could be required to work on study skills that might enhance their chances of succeeding. Success rates of students who participate in this more creative academic probation might be compared to other probationary students so we can learn whether our theory based intervention works.

Kathleen Manning (1996) cautions us not to abandon student affairs responsibilities in our enthusiasm for the new educational mandate; our role not only complements the academic mission but is essential to higher education's mission. In our roles we can be supportive and collaborative as we work to construct learning communities on our campuses. Elizabeth Blake (1996) provides for us a description of some of the obstacles to such collaboration: differing personal styles, distinctions between formal and other kinds of learning, faculty valuing of intellectual independence, and differing perceptions in power between student affairs and academic affairs. She cautions us to keep these obstacles in mind as we: work to defend the student affairs culture within our institutions, work with students to help them appreciate differences between academic and student affairs values, and develop a productive dialogue on our campuses that sharpens academic/student affairs contrasts in order to see their mutually shaping values.

Both thinking of students holistically and using theories of learning can provide us with cues for linking student affairs to learning both inside and outside the classroom. As advisors, leaders, and guides, we establish contexts within which the learning of the classroom can crystallize. Because learning takes place at the intersection of people's past lives and the sociocultural milieu in which they find themselves (Jarvis, 1992), we can help establish contexts that promote learning. College students have experienced much of their lives in the classroom. The milieu in which they live is a colorful combination of social, athletic, academic, and artistic events, all of which often provide meaning for their classroom learning.

Theories of learning and broadened approaches to partnerships with academic enterprises on campus could possibly help us in those discussions. And following Heath and McLaughlin's advice, we might make greater efforts to evaluate such learning experiences as evidence of the 'authenticity' of college students' learning.

Thirteen years ago Bob Shaffer (1984) described critical dimensions for student affairs as we moved toward the end of the millennium. Much of his advice, relevant then, seems equally relevant today as we close the millennium. He discussed budget cuts that he predicted would only worsen, forecast increases in nontraditional and diverse students causing increased demands on student affairs resources, and predicted increasing scrutiny regarding the value of traditional student affairs roles. He encouraged student affairs to take a more active role in the development of students' values, life goals, and leadership skills; to emphasize educational and vocational planning for students; to develop conflict resolution skills for all on campus; and to adopt more of a cooperative relationship based on trust and self directed growth for individuals. Finally, he enjoined us to work toward motivating students, creating social awareness, and building concern for social issues.

Robert Shaffer worried for us that if we maintained our thrust as "legalistic, bureaucratic keeper(s) of the status quo" that we would not be worthy of institutional resources expended on student affairs. Robert Shaffer as seer served the student affairs profession well. And while we have made great strides toward the needs and the efforts that he described, more can be done. The previous chapters describe new ways of looking at what now can be described (14 years later) as old problems.

References

Blake, E. S. (1996). The Yin and Yang of Student Learning in College. *About Campus: Enriching the Student Learning Experience*, *1*(4), 4–9.

Delandshere, G., and Petrosky, A. R. (1994). Capturing teachers' knowledge: Performance assessment. *Educational Researcher*, *23*(5), 11–18.

Erwin, T. D. (1991). *Assessing student learning and development*. San Francisco: Jossey-Bass.

Heath, S. B., and McLaughlin, M. W. (1994). Learning for anything everyday. *Journal of Curriculum Studies*, *26*, 471–489.

Hutchings, P. (1992). The assessment movement and feminism: Connection or collision. In T. Musil (ed.), *Students at the Center: Feminist Assessment*. Washington, D.C.: Association of American Colleges.

Jarvis, P. (1992). *Paradoxes of learning: On becoming an individual in society*. San Francisco: Jossey-Bass.

Manning, K. (1996). Contemplating the Myths of Student Affairs. *NASPA Journal*, *34*(1), 36–46.

Mentkowski, M. and Doherty, A. (1984). Abilities that last a lifetime: Outcomes of the Alverno experience. *American Association for Higher Education Bulletin*, *36*, 5–6, 11–14.

Shaffer, R. H. (1984). Critical Dimensions of Student Affairs in the Decades Ahead. *Journal of College Student Personnel*, *25*(2), 112–114.

About the Contributors

Frances Stage is Professor of Educational Leadership and Policy Studies at Indiana University–Bloomington. Stage teaches graduate courses in higher education. Her research focus is on learning college mathematics and on student success in mathematics and science majors. She was a winner of the Association for the Study of Higher Education's "Promising Scholar" award and Indiana University's "Outstanding Young Researcher" award, and the American College Personnel Associations "Annuit Coeptis" award for contributions to the profession through research and writing. Stage is the author or editor of nine books focusing on college student outcomes and learning.

Lemuel W. Watson is Dean of Academic Support, Heartland Community College, Bloomington, Illinois and former Associate Professor of Higher Education and Student Affairs in the Department of Educational Administration and Foundations at Illinois State University. He has degrees from the University of South Carolina, Ball State University, and Indiana University. Watson has experiences within the area of student affairs, business affairs, and academic affairs. He has received awards for his teaching style and compassion in the classroom. As a scholar, his research focuses on educational outcomes (K-12 and Postsecondary), sociocultural developmental issues, assessment, and faculty development.

Michael J. Cuyjet is Associate Professor in the Educational and Counseling Psychology Department at the University of Louisville, where he is coordinator of the college student personnel program. Prior to that appointment, he served more than twenty years as a student affairs professional in student activities and general student affairs administration at several universities.

Leanne Lewis Newman is a doctoral student in the college student personnel program at the University of Louisville. She has previously worked professionally at four colleges and universities, primarily in the student life and residence life areas. Her research interest is in success of minority college students.

Dr. Magdalena H. de la Teja is Assistant Provost for Student Development at Austin Community College in Austin, Texas. She earned a Ph.D. in Higher Education Administration and law degree from the University of Texas at Austin. Formerly, she served as Assistant to the Vice President for Student Affairs at U.T. at Austin and practiced law for three years. She is National Chair of the Two Year and Community Colleges Network of the National Association of Student Personnel Administrators and serves as a Visiting Committee Member of the Southern Association of Colleges and Schools. Dr. de la Teja has published articles on various education issues.

Diane Kramer is a Licensed Professional Counselor and has been a member of the faculty at Austin Community College since 1978. She established the A.C.C. Support Center which provides social services and textbook/child care assistance to non-traditional students. In addition to counseling students in educational, career, and personal areas, she has taught in the Human Development and Psychology departments.

Patricia Muller is a doctoral candidate in Higher Education at Indiana University. She received her masters in college student personnel administration and has worked in the areas of student activities and community service, including serving as Coordinator for Community Service and Service-learning at Indiana University. In addition, Muller has published and presented on learning theories, service-learning, and Paulo Freire's concientization. Currently, she is engaged in research concerning women and science achievement.

Melvin C. Terrell has served as Vice President for Student Affairs and Professor of Counselor Education at Northeastern Illinois University (NEIU) since 1988. In 1993, in recognition of his leadership potential, the American Council on Education awarded Dr. Terrell a one-year fellowship at Florida State University. Dr. Terrell was also the first minority to receive the NASPA Region IV-East Scott Goodnight Award for Outstanding Service as a Dean. He has been affiliated with a number of professional organizations, most notably the National Association of Student Personnel Administrators (NASPA) and the American College Personnel Association (ACPA), and has served on the Media Board of ACPA and the Editorial Board of the Journal of College Student Development.

M. Lee Upcraft is a Research Associate in the Center for the Study of Higher Education, Assistant Vice-President Emeritus for Student Affairs, and Affiliate Professor Emeritus in Higher Education at Penn State University. Dr. Upcraft is a Senior Scholar of the American College Personnel Association, and has received several awards from professional associations for his contributions to higher education.